PUSHING OUT THE BOAT - Issue 14

Foreword by Wayne Price

Pushing Out the Boat is so much more than just another literary magazine: well into its second decade now (far outlasting the average lifespan of the species) its 14 issues comprise an extraordinary and beautifully produced treasure house of new writing and art. Part of its unique value is that it provides North-East Scotland with a journal to be proud of, one that any other region would envy, acting as a vital inspiration for emerging (and of course established) writers and artists making their own contributions to a line of local brilliance. Another, equally vital, aspect of its quality is its complete and refreshing lack of parochialism. From its earliest days, the magazine has been welcoming to an extraordinary breadth of artistic approaches and inspirations: visual as much as literary, rural as much as urban, experimental as much as traditional, regional as much as international. All tones of voice can be found here, and all shades of vision; the one common denominator is quality.

It's very fitting that this year's cover art has been donated by no less an artist than 2016 V&A Prize winner (and ex-Artist in Residence at Peacock Visual Arts) Tom Hammick. I can't think of a better word than lyrical to describe the haunting blend of narrative and dreamlike imagery in his luminous print. A beautiful vision of lovers 'pushing out the boat', it's also a work, as the artist himself explains below, that draws its inspirations from the operas of Europe and the art of Edo-period Japan. Like the magazine itself, then, it reminds us that the best art is beyond simple borders and boundaries, always teasing our imaginations to cross over from one form of expression, one way of telling, one way of seeing, to another. What could be more appropriate as a gateway to Issue 14?

In an age of increasing intolerance and even contempt for diversity and open-heartedness, *Pushing Out the Boat*, like Hammick's print, is a reminder of the power and special value of creative expression itself, free of snobbery, prejudice and narrowness of any kind. It's a remarkable tribute to each contributor, emerging or well known, working in whatever mode or form, united by a love of craft and creative expression; and a tribute to the volunteers who, in its production and marketing, make the whole thing possible for the people of North-East Scotland and far beyond, year after year, triumphantly.

Dr Wayne Price is the author of the short story collection Furnace, *the novel* Mercy Seat *(both published by Freight Books) and the Laureate's Choice poetry pamphlet* Fossil Record *(smith|doorstop). He has lived and worked in Aberdeen since 2002 where he teaches English and Creative Writing at the University of Aberdeen.*

~~~

The artist Tom Hammick's inspiration for the cover image: *'Violetta and Alfredo's Escape* was inspired by a residency I had as Artist in residence at ENO. This woodcut came from listening and watching their production of Traviata many times. I wanted to give Violetta a break, and somehow enable her and Alfredo to at least attempt to escape from the cruelty and stringent morals of the bourgeois society that separated them. Here they are in suburban bliss, somewhere I imagine upstream on the Thames! (Rather than in the Parisian outskirts.) Their domestic sojourn happens in my picture in a post war detached span house, cosy, small, simple. The garden is a take on a print by my hero Hiroshige, but the passing of time is indicated by some trees in blossom, some in full leaf and others as skeletal winter shapes.'

Tom Hammick is an artist based in East Sussex and London. 'Moved by the minutiae in life, he reflects on man's place in the world, his seductive landscapes metaphors for the human condition... the work sharing sensibilities with contemporary narrative forms.' (See Page 3 for more information about the artist and the image.)

CONTENTS

CONTENTS

Front & Back Covers based on an image by Tom Hammick: Violetta & Alfredo's Escape 2016, edition variable reduction woodcut, edition of 12, 160 x 120 cm © Tom Hammick, courtesy Hammick Editions (www.hammickeditions.com) & Flowers Gallery (www.flowersgallery.com).

A Senior Lecturer in Fine Art, Painting and Printmaking at the University of Brighton, Visiting Lecturer Fine Art at University of Ulster, and at NSCAD University, Tom Hammick's work is found in many major public and corporate collections including the British Museum, V & A, Bibliotheque Nationale de France, Deutsche Bank, Yale Centre for British Art, and The Library of Congress, Washington DC.

Street in Central HK

Jane Pettigrew
Colour / Watercolour
2D 370 x 470 mm

Joke

you say have we heard the one about
the shrinking cat?

the vet's diagnosis:
too much condensed milk

you're shrinking too
but your diagnosis isn't funny at all

tell us another one

Mandy Haggith

Longannet

A heron stalks its own reflection
in the mud at low tide,
and all the while Grangemouth, roaring.

A Bay Window Drops from the Second Storey

As if all the wires were cut at once.
The dull surprise of disconnection;
nothing
means anything at all.

This is how she feels,
spoon halfway to her mouth,
staring at the hole in her wall where
a window used to be.

The shock is not in the crash,
nor in the sudden loss of her reading nook.
It is in the face of the man across the road.
He looks the same,

a pair of waving hands
bobbing on the horizon.

Nathan Breakenridge

The Candlelight Patrol

Saudi Arabia: 12 January 1991 / 26 Jumada 1411

Nine o'clock and three days before the Gulf War starts. Rob urges Cilla, his black Labrador, into the back of the patrol car, settles her on the old yellow carpet, and drives out of Acacia Court on the Candlelight Patrol. Swinging right past Banyan and Cactus Courts, he joins Perimeter Road and cruises beside the high chain link fence of the Airbase, headlights searching for breaks in the wire. Even at this time, the oil camp's streets and courtyards are deserted - people huddled in their homes waiting for the next news bulletin, the first Scud Alerts to start wailing out. But soon he's feeling comfortable inside the patrol car, with Mother's Easy Listening station muttering over the radio and Cilla, stretched out on the backseat, shifting occasionally to raise her head, look around, and settle back again.

As he leaves, CNN is reporting that James Baker, the US Secretary of State, is visiting the Airbase checking the preparations for war. Now, beyond the perimeter fence, the Base lies waiting, brooding through the wintery night, and gathering itself for attack. On this side, the oil camp's courtyards are silent, oblivious to what Rob knows is the frenzied activity opposite - trucks shuttling aviation fuel and supplies along the feeder roads, the candy men loading helicopter gunships and planes with munitions, pilots being briefed for reconnaissance flights over Iraq and occupied Kuwait. Yet despite the sharp silhouettes of hardened shelters, the pinpricks of light in the gloom marking the giant Galaxy transports, that feverish activity is difficult to imagine here as he slowly cruises along by the perimeter fence.

First on his checklist, the new mobile homes. No lights in the cabin windows as he drives slowly round Canyon Circle. The nurses and medical staff living there were only recently evacuated, but already the parched gardens and sand accumulating on the front steps threaten the return of the surrounding desert. If Saddam's Scuds get through, this whole camp will empty and the desert sands blow in over everything. But that's alarmist - the British and American embassies say it won't happen.

He turns back onto Perimeter Road and drives down towards the Utilities Department, its illuminated Pepsi vending machine standing guard outside the office building. Further along, the still waters of the sewage treatment ponds glisten under yellow sodium lights. The luxuriant grass around the ponds was recently mown and he remembers reading in the company newspaper about a crazy golf competition there, an event designed to publicise Mother's new sanitation system.

Next stop the AAA garage. Old cars and trucks are parked haphazardly outside, abandoned when their owners fled after the invasion of Kuwait and threats to invade Saudi. He pulls into the space between a white Ford Transit and a Toyota pick-up with an old mattress and black garbage bags dumped in the back. Facing the padlocked gate, his headlights beam through the wire mesh onto the garage forecourt, the vehicles parked for repair and the inspection ramp curving up into the night sky. He gets out to scan the area, checking for suspicious movements beyond the beam of his headlights. The smell of gasoline that always hangs over camp is usually strongest here, but the chill wind from the sea is dispersing it, threatening more rain and discomfort for the troops camped up north near the Kuwaiti border. It's the coldest and wettest Saudi winter he can remember; he zips up his Loss Prevention windcheater and pulls the baseball cap firmly down on his head.

No lights are showing in the garage workshops where the remaining Filipino mechanics devote evenings and weekends to their private business, repairing Westerners' cars and four-wheel drives. Behind the garage he can see the junk yard's piles of rusting parts, two large metal containers parked up against the fence. "It's a weak point," Rick, the big American security boss, had warned on his orientation drive round. "Better stay alert."

But no suspicious movements. He reverses back onto the road, driving down towards the grove of palm trees screening the agricultural research station. He cruises into the car park, headlights washing over the dimly lit plant nursery and greenhouses, where tomatoes and cucumbers grow in plastic tubes without soil, sustained only by running water enriched with plant food. The tops of palm trees are swaying in the breeze, the car warm and comfortable inside, and he winds down the driver's window. Already he's feeling tired, needing this blast of cold air.

Past the agricultural station, the road turns sharp right, heading towards the lights of bachelor housing. But he drives straight on following the high chain-link fence. With a bump, he leaves the tarmac onto an unlit dirt track used by garbage trucks going to the landfill pits beyond the lagoon. He drives more cautiously, headlights scanning the rough track and manoeuvring between potholes. Before the invasion, this wasteland with its mounds of rubble was a testing ground for teenagers racing BMXs and dirt bikes. After the invasion, most kids were evacuated with their mothers, back to homes around the world. How many will return? And will Fiona, his wife, ever return now that she's back home?

Headlights pierce the gloom and a US army Humvee, with a searchlight and machine gun mounted on top, bounds along the track on the other side of the fence. Spotting Rob's white patrol car, the base guards flash their lights, acknowledging their common purpose. They're heading towards the Patriot battery hidden among the small limestone *jebels* and waiting to shoot down any missiles attacking the Base. The Pentagon has spent billions of dollars on anti-missile systems but will this Patriot missile work? At first the Americans and British said that Saddam's Scuds wouldn't get through, but now they say they'll shoot them down.

He parks and lets Cilla jump out to roam around for a few minutes. Leaning forward into the breeze, he walks up a small *jebel*, a rocky perch overlooking the Airbase, where he can smoke a cigarette and perhaps spot James Baker's Air Force plane on the tarmac. Ten years since he stopped smoking, but for this time and place he's awarded himself the luxury of just one Marlboro cigarette each night.

Lighting up, he savours the deliciously illicit taste, this moment saved for tranquillity, and looks across the Base - the shapes of hardened shelters and barracks stretching into the distance, and the low moaning vibration of generators carried on the wind. It feels like he's living next door to a friendly giant who's kindly offered to take care of him. Or a mass murderer, whose surreptitious movements disturb him during the night but to whom, when they meet in the morning, he waves cheerfully on the way to work.

No sign of James Baker's plane – perhaps he's already left. So what can he think about tonight to while away the hours? Football? He and Alex, his teenage son, went to Pittodrie on Boxing Day and saw the Dons beat St Mirren 1-0. But after New Year they lost to Dundee - forget Miller and Jess, they aren't going to win the League this year. Maybe he should think about finances – now that they've repaid the mortgage, perhaps he needs to save for retirement? Since he came to Saudi, he's focused only on the money. But isn't it time to face more basic, more disturbing questions? Like what's kept him here and brought him back to patrol this perimeter fence, waiting for the Gulf war to begin?

~

After dinner, on his last night at home, he sat drinking coffee with Fiona and Alex round the kitchen table.

"Why are you going back Dad?" Alex demanded.

He began rationalising his decision – people at work depended on him, he wouldn't be dictated to by Saddam Hussein, the media were exaggerating the danger of Scuds, gas and chemical weapons...

"Cut the bullshit, Dad," Alex broke in. "Is it the money? So how much do you earn?"

He wouldn't answer directly: but when his son asked if it was over twenty thousand, he nodded. "Over thirty thousand?" When he nodded again, Alex conceded, "Suppose you've got to go back then."

Their discussion dissipated over more coffee but Fiona hadn't joined in the questioning. He was conscious of her strained expression, her determination to let him make his own decision, no matter how wrong it might be and how ill she felt. But how ill was she? He'd been reluctant to inquire too deeply as she might flare up. She'd gone to see the doctor about headaches and depression and returned with some pills. Presumably they'd work – they had before.

But in the end, it was always money. Money had brought him to Saudi and in a few months he'd complete ten years and qualify for full severance. One month's pay for each year of service shone like the Holy Grail before him. "I'm coming back after ten," he'd promised Fiona, kissing her goodbye at Aberdeen airport. "Only a few months to go."

~

Crushing his cigarette into the sand, he strolls down the bluff to the patrol car and opens the back door to let Cilla jump inside. On the radio, Phil Collins is singing about something in the air tonight, as Rob checks in with the Big House.

"Assalam alikum. Welcome back to Paradise my friend." Abdul Karim - Al to his Western colleagues - greets him through the crackling, his Texan accent a legacy of detective training in Dallas. "How's the family? You have good Christmas?"

"Good. So how's your family, Al?"

"Zain. I take to Riyadh for safety. Only strong men stay for this war *sideeki."*

But Al's usual good humour sounds constrained. Is Rick, his American boss, in the Control Room listening in?

"You see Mr Baker yet?" Al asks. "He's visiting the guys at the Base."

"No. Nothing to report. All's quiet here."

"Alhamdullilah. Good to hear you're back my friend. But be careful out there, "Al concludes, with his familiar caution from the roll-call sergeant in *Hill Street Blues*.

Time now to drive to the lagoon created to drain off and evaporate the camp's sewage effluent. Scrubby tamarisk trees and bushes screen this man-made oasis where in the evening birdwatchers and photographers come to spy on migrant birds. After a day's work and in the settling cool of the jogging and dog-walking hour, the lagoon appears a romantic and peaceful place, skirted by reeds and illuminated by the setting sun. But it's close to the Patriot base - terrorists could do some damage, Rick had warned.

Rob bumps along the dirt track towards the trees, parks his car before the thicket of tamarisks, and steps out into the whine of mosquitoes already gathering round his head. Snakes lurk in the long grass so he puts Cilla on the lead and, his flashlight beaming the way ahead, walks down the sandy jogging track. Halfway round the lagoon the shrubs grow more dense and sheltered from the cold wind; he halts and plays out the lead for Cilla to snuffle round and pee in the bushes. He listens to the sound of the reeds shifting with the breeze, breathing in and out, proving the sheer determination of nature in this barren place.

He pulls on the lead but Cilla resists, wanting to stay longer; giving way, he decides he's got time to think. Here, stranded in the middle of his life and facing this approaching war, he should decide what he's going to do. Alex has graduated from university, the mortgage is paid, and he's 45 years old. He could go back to working in Aberdeen: at Christmas the city seemed prosperous. Maybe there are job opportunities like Fiona says, but he's almost ten years older, and his CV shows he's been out of the country too long. Or should he carry on working here, saving as much as possible so he can retire with Fiona? A depressing thought, but this approaching war could change his life.

He pulls Cilla back from the bushes and they follow the jogging track round the other side of the lagoon. It's brighter here with light from the courtyards of bachelor housing shining across the barren spray fields where underground sprinklers periodically spurt out surplus effluent. The street and house lights snap out, the road and courtyards lost in blackness, as if someone's pulled a master switch. They said there'd be blackouts when the war started – perhaps this is just practice. But feeling more alone beside the lagoon, he moves his flashlight round and pulls Cilla to him as he hurries back to the patrol car.

Next on his checklist is the derelict electrical substation, standing isolated in the wasteland like an abandoned Second World War pillbox. Power lines droop down from the telegraph poles spaced along the track towards it. But he's only driven for a few minutes when a large boulder appears unexpectedly in the headlights, barring the way forward. Mounds of dirt and building rubble border the track but this seems deliberately placed to stop a car driving on. The boulder looks too heavy to move so he edges his patrol car off the track onto the sand and dirt. Immediately he feels the vehicle sinking, the wheels slipping out of control. He stops. There's been heavy rain over the last few days and he could get bogged down. Shifting into reverse and pressing the accelerator, he struggles to back up onto more solid ground, sweat gathering on his forehead, droplets trickling down under his arms as the engine revs. At last, the wheels jerk back onto firmer ground and he can straighten up.

He decides to walk to the substation: he puts Cilla on the lead, takes the heavy flashlight from the passenger seat and steps out of the car's warm security. His headlights shine ahead, picking out more rubble on the track, scraps of litter blown against the substation's wire fence.

Something shifts, a flicker of movement by the wire fence, and in the corner of his eye he sees something. He halts, shining his light around the substation, but everything seems still. He steps forward, scanning the area, giving an intruder the opportunity to run. Still nothing. Conscious of leaving the safety of his patrol car further behind, he advances, planting his feet firmly on the ground. Cilla's barking, pulling him forward - a flicker in his vision, and the flashlight almost catches a low shape fleeing across the waste ground, then lost behind mounds of rubble.

Shocked, he yanks Cilla back. A wild dog or maybe one of the desert foxes that scavenge round the waste dumps? Or a man? Could it have been a man crouching low as he ran for cover? A man escaping from behind the substation? Cilla's still barking, standing up on her back legs and straining to run forward. Rob stays still, forcing himself to calm down, control his breathing and listen into the night sounds – but there's only the steady chirping of the cicada, the wind's low moaning over the wasteland. Was it someone running, hiding behind the mounds of rubble, and escaping now across the spray-fields?

He advances and slowly walks round the substation, examining the chain link fence and holding Cilla close, alert to any movement in the shadows. His flashlight shines through the wire, sweeping round to the grey metal door of the control building and a DANGER sign - a white skull and crossbones and electrical shock markers radiating out. Below is KEEP AWAY in Arabic and English. More Arabic letters are scrawled in white paint on the door and a large rusty padlock hangs safely in place. A polystyrene cup lies trapped under the fence, some flattened Pepsi and Dr Pepper cans gleaming in the light and a Domino's pizza box has blown against the gate. People have eaten here. But recently? No damage to the wire, no sign of anyone breaking in. Maybe he's getting over-excited, imagining things.

A last sweep of the area with his flashlight and all's clear. He walks back along the track to his patrol car, feeling like a returning hero bathed in welcoming headlights. He opens the door for Cilla to jump inside and settles back into the warmth and Easy Listening sound of John Denver taking him back where he belongs. Past eleven o'clock and time to check in again with the Big House.

"*Assalam alikum,*" Al greets him. "Where are you my friend? Anything to report?"

"I'm near the electrical sub-station. The lights are out in this area."

"*Mafi muskallah*, no problem my friend – we're testing the system.'"

"Think I saw a desert fox or dog, something by the substation." Rob almost jokes about Cilla chasing it, but then remembers dogs aren't allowed on patrol. If Rick or Al found out...

"Sure it's an animal?" Al's on the alert. "What did you see?"

Rob isn't sure but if he says that, they'll drive round and catch him with Cilla.

"OK, calm down Al. Four legs not two," he jokes.

A sudden eruption. Cilla cowers on the back seat and, even with his hands clasped over his ears, Rob recoils at the shriek and reverberation as jets rise in formation over the perimeter fence and burst into the air. He watches four heavily laden planes climb and recede into the distance, the gold and purple flare of afterburners fading behind into the night sky. Only three days left before the war starts.

Peter Sheal

This is the opening chapter of a novel written from the perspective of a Scot working in the Saudi Arabian oil industry.

The Retention Bonus

That wee man in that Middlesbrough pub
has half the crew on tick, ticked off
in his black book and now the payment's due.

Bad weather, piss-poor planning and excessive rust, they say.
The flotel wallows in September gales, the bridge is up
and you sit idle as your interest swells.   The bonus is deferred.

No consultation.   And no questions asked.   Stick to the Christmas club
next time, the wife's menodge. It seemed a safe-bet then. The ten percent
lump-sum on top and just for staying on till sail-away.

Their share-price rocks upon the project milestone.
But no explaining that to his black book
that says the money's owed with compound interest.

The markets get results from either end no matter how
you plead and reason, beg, protest you can't
climb back into that chopper with a broken leg.

John Bolland

The Type

Roddy - with his leather trousers, prince-albert and a diver
tattooed on each buttock - owned a pianola and a burgundy
Rolls Royce we'd roll down to the chip-shop in for chips.

There was a lot of dope back then before the Kielland sank. St Swithin Street.
Where divers woke with Egg upon their face and Helen cooked us breakfast
in her tee-shirt.   Just her tee-shirt. Ned got off

the Piper. Didn't wait to die. Climbed down to the 40 foot and jumped.
While Raymond (and his girlfriend) robbed an Opco - that went sour.
And Nicky, blonde and buxom and a first - a lady diver -

was always getting just one trip with Comex, the Piranha Brothers or Subsea
to see what she was made of. Roddy'd ask
on those few nights we shared the attic room high up - up in the attic, just we two –

if I was sleeping with my back against the wall? I always did
(naive for all the difference it would make). One Tuesday night we shared
Vivaldi's *Gloria* and something he'd picked up in Singapore

the last time he came through. *The Four Last Songs.* Years later,
someone said he was the type. The type - they said - that would get up
one morning, put pistol in his mouth and...

The Kielland sank and Piper burned and now the rest rust through a bitter age
the dark sea dragging at their spider decks. St Swithin Street.
The music fades. I see I am the type...

John Bolland

What Do You Give Someone With Tinnitus?

Gammy loved birds.

As her birthday, as Christmas approached, we grandkids would marshal resources to search the five and dime for some sort of tchotchke with a bird. Then one lucky year someone found a porcelain bell with a bird decal and thereafter bells were the surefire gift for Gammy.

After Papa died Gammy moved from Palmdale to Magalia just a mile or two above Paradise. Diana and I would visit her in that lovely little house among the trees. The three of us sat together next to her purring wood stove and I paid her a compliment on her collection of bells, crystal, metal, clay, displayed around the room.

I can only remember my Gammy swearing once: *If somebody gives me another goddamned bell that I have to dust, I'm going to...*

Ding!

Robert Haycock

Okanagan

For weeks, the bush fire's been burning.
August plums smolder in the orchards.
The ochre flesh bursts through the purple skins,
sends the over-ripe scent up the valley,
through the mosquito screen
into our bedroom, where desire ends.
Our bodies dry from the heat, smoke
paling the sage hills gray.

Lily Gontard

After the Flood - the Dead Tree

Nicola Chambury
Colour / Etching
2D 600 x 155 mm

Three North East Vignettes - 2016

1 Rubislaw Hole

And here he is again. Determined now. Paint flaking from the chipboard shuttering. Behind the shuttering is the fence and then the bushes and beyond all that - the hole. He can't decide if all these barriers are intended for his protection or for theirs. Or are they meant to keep the hole a secret? Though why would it remain a secret? It is just a hole. The hole the city came from.

The city - stacked high walls of granite marking out the floor-plan of their lives, a labyrinth of sorts - and built to last. A statement of intent, these granite buildings. A statement meant to be endured. The incomers mutter that this slump will be the end of it.

He keyed the Porsche that morning. It wasn't clear how that would help but let them repossess it now.

The shuttering is shabby, flaking and de-layering here and there. A pen-knife can easily prise a panel from the supporting batten, opening up a space. This space again. And then the iron railing and the bushes, then the hole. He looked it up. Six million tonnes of granite stolen. Ninety metres deep.

It is Friday - not so much flex- as sag-Friday these days. Take your time, they say. Go slow. For God's sake, finish fuck all. For when we're finished that will be the end of it.

He believes all of the granite came out of the hole. The modern buildings ranged behind him now were never meant to last. Concrete and I-beams. Four floors high and mostly up for lease. Britoil had its office here, back in the day. BNOC. Forward-leaning premises built right beside the hole, asserting national interest in futures yet-unmapped. Wealth and riches. Governance and stewardship. A farm-in to the greed of others. Bigged up beside the hole. Some say the last blast was in '71. Others insist it was '79. The latter made more sense to him these days. The year of Thatcher. The year of the first referendum. The year the fire sale started.

The railing still has spikes along the top. It's a delicate manoeuvre but he wouldn't want to just impale himself upon the fence, neither here nor there, and be found later impotently bleeding. Too emblematic. Pinned there struggling. BOHICA management and a free North Face fleece with each new life-choice. Get over it.

And he does. The bushes then the hole.

'I still had a job on Friday.' How many times has he said it these last two years? And now he'd never say the words again. He should never have cut back from malts to blends. A stupid gesture in the scheme of things. Skimming off the top.

Right down the passenger side door. Two long scores. Fuck them.

On the bushes, hips and haws and rowan berries. Spots of blood hanging heavy on the boughs, amidst the thorns, against the grey sky. Would it have been better to wait for finer weather? The awkwardness of the situation. He has never done anything like this before and, by definition, he never will again. So best get it right.

They sold the national interest to BP. They say that to this day you can tell a Britoil man by his employee number. Those few who still remain. Easy to decode. Picked up in a life-raft. What does that say about his seamanship? But his Opco days are long past. Long past.

First early retirement then contracting. Easy money - take the package then come back. But how it bleeds away. How they bled it all away. And now the hole.

He presses himself against the thin trunk of a rowan tree and gazes down. This is where it all comes from. A hole. The origin of the world. Eventually the hole was exhausted.   Did it get too deep? Did it run out of stone? What tipped the economics? The water level rising? Always that dynamic. Flood fill. Water. Stone. Hole. And the fourth element. Fire. Isn't it? We live by fire.

It is deeper than he thought. Deeper than it looks from the air as the London flight tracks low across the city.   And then beneath the surface how much more?

He hesitates then drops the laptop case and all the files and datasets and documents and emails. It turns - once, twice - before it finds the surface. Like a falling man. That far then. Two turns. All gone. A life's work.

He turns again. His trouser leg catches on the railing spike.   He finds he cannot free himself.

2 Milonga

This is simple. *Abrazo cerrado*. Though nothing is simple.

His right arm stretches behind her and pulls her towards him; his left, lifting her hand high, steadies her as she over-balances towards him. In a moment the music will begin again and he will move. She is older than he is. Perhaps a decade older. Her teeth are yellow. Her lipstick a little too pale for her complexion. He has seen her at the factory.

At the first note his left foot slips forward and a little left, turning her as he pushes her back across the polished floor of the church hall.   He scans ahead, tracking the other couples who shuffle and clump, impeding his glide. Her feet struggle to find the steps as he drives her back but she is one of those who is content to be led. He pushes her around the floor. Turning her. Twisting her.

She packs prawns. That is where he has seen her before. In the packing area, in a white coat, a hair net under her hard hat. Yellow gumboots. Now, in a tight black dress, high heels, she is trying to be serious. She is trying too hard. He turns her sharply to the left. She raises her right foot and, sensing her ambition, he pauses as she attempts a *gancho*, kicking him on the shin. She smiles.

There are stages in the process. The sorting. The shelling. The packing. The shelling is the worst job. The prawns' fragile bodies resist evisceration, but ineffectually, their thorns and spines inflicting tiny lacerations into which the brine seeps. But nothing in their lives accommodates this vast dismembering, the powerful twist that tears the head-part from the tail, rubs off the legs then husks the flesh from its shell. Ten thousand prawns a shift. More on a good day. The bodies on the line sorting, shelling, packing till the catch is cleared and stowed into the lorries parked outside the shed. The lorries bound for Vigo, Barcelona, San Sebastián. Home.

He slips his right foot against her right, pressing against her insole as he slips her foot in a *barrida*, parting her thighs. Her smile seems less apologetic. The smell of fish on his raw fingers. Salt and death.

The music stops. He lets her go. He waits. She bobs her head. Perhaps in gratitude. Perhaps not.

He places his left hand against the palm of his new partner. She is taller than the one before. Bony and angular like a hake. Her breath smells of cigarettes and rum. She smiles just like the rest. His shin still aches. He steps forward.

3 The Lady Who Lunched

This hotel has been closing down for years - yet here she is, contemplating the chocolate eclair, admiring the swirl of colour the barman has patterned on the crema of her coffee - like a love-heart or a quim.

They will never sell the hotel now. That moment has past. Now it must be forever what it was - dilapidating.

She smiles at that. Can that be a verb? I dilapidate... you dilapidate...? And surely it would need to be reflexive. As in the French: *Je me dilapide...* Or something.

She bites into the eclair and the squidge of cream that oozes from the edge collects on the fine hairs above her lipstick. She sips her coffee. One day he will come back. One day the fair Evgenya will grow fat. One day the arse will fall out of his world.

For herself - she will never put on more than half a stone. She will make sure of it. Let Evgenya pad those hips of hers (she is stalking her on Facebook). Let them revel in the sensuous pleasure of her Slavic curves until she tips over the edge onto that slippery slope and slurries to the bottom.

For herself, she'll wait here and dilapidate gracefully. Just like this hotel. She decides she likes that word - dilapidate - and delicately wipes the froth from her upper lip. Changed days. Coffee and an eclair. Prosecco on a Saturday. The dust of icing sugar where once she wore cocaine.

Her friend is late. This is what you settle for. Lateness. Negligence. A certain disarray. But there is time. None of them is going anywhere soon. And who would want to live in Aktau anyway?

She takes a second bite of the eclair.

It is surprising that the hotel gym is often empty these afternoons. Gym membership must be viewed as a luxury for the over-leveraged, she supposes. 'A false economy', she wants to tell the thirty-something mums. Incompatible with the 'good idea' of daddy going on a rota somewhere. 'Give yourself a fighting chance, my dear.' But she says nothing. She likes the quiet. Cher on her headphones drowning out the grind of the step machine.

It's handy that they are building the by-pass at last. Just what the town will need a few years down the way - a by-pass.

Their former marital home teeters on the edge of the mud and the bustle waiting for it all to end. She bought herself a telescope just like in Frasier and watches the workmen of a morning. How slowly things progress. How little seems to be achieved. And she wonders if that is what his life was like all those years when she thought he was bustling. Was he, all that time, plodding back and forth, looking for that misplaced tool or a signature from someone inexplicably off-site? Had that been all he was before he met Evgenya?

Dilatory. Her friend is dilatory, she decides and wonders if that is related in some way to the word 'dilapidated'. Sets off on a tour of words begin with 'dil'. Diligent. Dil... dil...? Choosing to avoid the obvious with a knowing smile. I didn't know, she tells herself. I swear I did not know. So how can I be knowing or complicit? That snatch of sensation. Snorting white powder through a £20 note in the ladies' loo. How could you have failed to notice?

'Easily distracted,' she tells herself and takes a third bite of the eclair. There is hardly any left. It is vexatious of her friend to be so late.

The last stump of the eclair smears wasted cream and Belgian chocolate fondant on the *faux chic* plate. 'Would she describe that as dilapidated?' she wonders. Ruined surely? It is a ruin. And yet there is still in that last mouthful the same sweetness, the same moist sensuous melting as in the first. It is what remains of it. That's all.

She pops it in her mouth and sucks the chocolate from her fingertips. 'All gone,' she tells herself, deciding she has waited long enough.

John Bolland

Moira Scicluna Zahra
Colour / Brush and Digital Colour
1794 x 2451 px

Oratorio

This morning, all around the camping field,
new-shorn sheep have treated us
to a rousing oratorio. *Baah* they go,
Nnn and *Meeeh,* then – towards
the denouement – *Beeeehh.*

Waiting in the queue for the showers,
a French camper talks about words
shared by Breton and Gaelic, and how
being brought up bilingually seems
to add to memory rather than diminish it.

Meanwhile, back in the field, a leading
sheep tenor is exposing its soul.
Beeh, it sings, *Meh*, and *Bah*, raising us up
with its joyful incomprehension.

Ian McDonough

Sappho Fragments

(on reading that some were found, written upon papyrus,
used for stuffing the mouths of mummified crocodiles.)

those things **W**e did,
in **O**ur youth
ca**R**e for best,
Do
mo**S**t harm

y**O**u came and
I was mad **F**or you

you coo**L**ed my
l**O**nging,
lo**V**ed
a littl**E** graceless

herald o**F**
sp**R**ing,
v**O**ice of longing,
loosener of li**M**bs

Troubles
Have
forgott**E**n

Me and
y**O**u
b**U**t
They
reac**H**
Stars -

the l**O**veliest
Flower -

I **C**annot
wo**R**k the
l**O**om
in time to **C**ome -
here n**O**w
the **D**elicate graces
w**I**th
beautifu**L**
lam**E**nt in
the mu**S**e's house

Neil Russell

Hands as Big as Dinner Plates

His name's Dai and he's as tall as a shut church door, his hands as big as dinner plates and his head as square as a dressed stone; and there was a time that his words, when he chose to speak, came out all spit and bellow and punch. Old women could not bring forth a civil 'Good morning' from him and the minister had given up trying to shake his hand after service and once had slapped him on the back instead, a warm and friendly gesture that he did not try a second time.

"God bless you, Dai," the minister used to say; he says 'God bless' to everyone and his dog, but there was a difference when he said it to Dai, like it was a duty and not something really meant, not back then.

Dai, all scowls and prickles back then and it seemed that he always had been that way, for as far back as memory goes, even to the child Dai was once. His life was a hard life, people said, and they shook their heads and felt briefly sorry for him. But then hadn't they had hard lives, too? And they at least could muster a smile on a sunny day or a dance come festival time or a song on their lips on church-Sundays.

He'd buried his mam when he was still young – that was sometimes said – and there was no da to speak of, at least none that stood up to own the boy; it might have been different with Dai if his mam had lived or if a da had stepped up. That was understood. Dai didn't open doors for no one and he didn't have 'please' or 'thank you' in his vocabulary and he kept himself to himself as much as any man can. The people shrugged and soon enough gave it little thought, for they had grown used to him.

And Dai, hadn't he worked breaking stone even when he was half the size he is now, and that's no easy job, his hands bearing callouses and the muscles of his arms pulled like rope when it ties fast a bull and the bull tugs and strains to be free. Dai bent a little also, with the effort, but not so it was remarked on. And bent enough so it was as if he always carried a weight on his own bullish shoulders, and he would take help from no one and that was understood also.

His job splitting stone was up at Carrew's quarry and he earned a penny more than most for the work that he did and a grudging respect from the men for his incomparable strength. Been there for years and years at Carrew's quarry and, though they'd tried at first, the other men learned to give Dai his own space, and so he was no more invited to Y Mochyn Du for a pint of ale at the end of a day's labouring, and no one made a gesture with the hands like pushing down bread before its second rise, or said to Dai, "Rest a minute, man, and sit down with us for a mug of strong tea and a bit biscuit, why don't you?"

So it was that Dai was alone – 'He lives alone and he'll dai alone' – and that was a joke in the village but one that dared not reach Dai's ears. Lived in the house his mam had lived in before and he kept it well enough, the frames of the windows painted each year and the front door, too, and the slumped slung stone step scrubbed clean as any other in the street, every Saturday Dai fallen to his knees with a bucket of water and soap and a hard bristle brush and elbow grease. And there were women who might have remarked on how good the house looked, like they did with new wives, which was only to encourage them, but they knew better than to do that with Dai.

The house had two bedrooms upstairs and a front room and a kitchen downstairs. And on Sundays Dai pulled the tin bath before the fire and he half-filled it with water hot enough to scald chickens out of their feathers. Took him half the afternoon, and there was a great deal of clattering as Dai shifted pots about the cooking range and rattled the poker in the grate and fetched coal to feed the fire and more water for his bath. Clean as a new pin he'd be after, though he was black still in the middle of his back where he could not reach. And his hair all slick and flat, and his cheeks as red as rash or raspberries. And Dai would take a turn around the town then, dressed up in his church-suit and his shoes buffed to a glossy shine, and all to announce his cleanness to the world. Then back to his house and the door shut hard and the week pulling to a close – Dai alone at the end of the day in his bed.

That's how it had been for the longest time and everyone thought that's how it would be till Dai was one day laid in the ground beside his mam and no one to say a prayer over him then, unless the minister took that as a duty, too. But the world can sometimes be stood on its head in an instant, and up can be down and down can be up, and so it was with Dai. Sudden as thunderclaps it was, and no change in the sky to show it was coming and nothing quite the same after.

See, no one had calculated on Dilys. Had not seen her casting her eyes at Dai in church when she should have been praying; nor seen her blush when he passed her in the Sunday-afternoon-street all dressed up to the nines and clean and pink, passing as brusque as a slapped wind but passing not without Dilys noticing; nor did anyone hear her sigh when she was by herself in the street again and Dai gone back indoors.

Dilys, herself as big as a milk cow, and she moved with slow heavy steps, lumbering; and chairs complained whenever she sat in them, even in church, and before God the people held their breath and prayed that wood could be as strong as stone or metal, just till Dilys rose again out of the pew and the congregation offered up a collective sigh of relief.

"Thanks be and bless you, Dilys," said the minister at the end of service – and maybe he, too, was thanking God that the pews had held – and he stroked her hand and patted her shoulder and he asked after how she was, smiling and nodding to her every word as if he was really listening. And the minister watched her walk away afterwards, her feet skipping almost, or walking as though her shoes hurt her feet or glass or fire was what she trod on, and all of her shook and rippled in wonderful places, and the minister smiled again and he licked his lips without knowing that he did.

And the men in Y Mochyn Du sometimes sucked their fingers and they said they wouldn't say no to Dilys if ever she asked, and they said as how Dilys was woman enough for any man and too much for most. And she was pretty as a painting, see, despite her size, her hair all glossy black as the wings of crows and her eyes blue as the high-summer sky and flecked with amber shards. She could light up a room just by being in it they said, or the street or anywhere, and in the dark of lights-out boys had dreams about her and what she looked like with no clothes on, and men had the same dreams except being men and not boys they knew what to do with a naked Dilys, or they dreamed that they did which amounts to the same thing.

And the village had not accounted for Dilys in their calculations of how the life of Dai would unfold. For Dilys one day walked straight into Dai's old house, his mam's house, without so much as knocking or waiting for an invitation, and that changed everything.

Dai and Dilys, Dilys and Dai, and they made love with the window open that first time, and such a noise they made of it that brought the women all into the street thinking there must be fighting going on. Brought the men out of Y Mochyn Du, too. And when they were done – Dilys and Dai – and a breathless quiet returned to the street, and the women crept back to their homes and the men to their drinks in Y Mochyn Du, well, there was a feeling then, under the laughter and behind the wagged fingers, a feeling of loss and gain, both at the same time. And the world was changed, and changed utterly and they did not straightaway know how, not any of them.

From that day to this, Dilys has belonged to Dai, and Dai has belonged to Dilys, and neither of them have ever been seen in church again, not even to be married; but they stop to pass the time of day with the minister, when they've a mind to, and they throw out cheery 'good mornings' to anyone who wants them and even to them that don't. And sometimes they take a drink in Y Mochyn Du, sitting at a table beside the frosted glass window, and they nod to the men at the bar, and the men are mindful of their 'p's and q's' then and no one spits on the floor and rude jokes are kept till after they've gone.

And Dilys and Dai, they never close their windows, not against wasps in autumn or frost in winter or the bite of midges in summer. Their windows thrown wide and always, and they never know shame and make love almost every day it seems and make it loud as bulls bellowing, and even on Sundays.

And though there's been a softening of Dai with his great 'good mornings' and his face all broken into smiles, and even though Dai is not really Dai anymore, not the Dai from before, not the Dai that was all prickles and scowls; still nor boys nor men dare to dream of Dilys without her clothes these days, for if they do there's always a stone-splitting Dai with his hands as big as dinner plates standing in the dark behind Dilys, and, well, you just never know with dreams.

Douglas Bruton

Up to my Neck

It's so lovely here
with my head in the sand
The grains tickle
my face in such a nice way
So cool
through scorched days warm
in iced nights

Of course
I made sure I found
some godforsaken patch
lost to all mankind
Imagine
my head unearthed by some spod
with a plastic bucket

I'm utterly alone
held close by a million billion grains
I made sure too
that my body won't give
the game away
It carries on in daily grind
really quite admirably

No one has yet noticed No one
Not one Nobody
No body Actually
these grains scratch
I feel a tad claustrophobic
Maybe I should stick my
neck out just a little

Maxine Rose Munro

Lone Boat, River Lossie

Creel on Lossie Beach

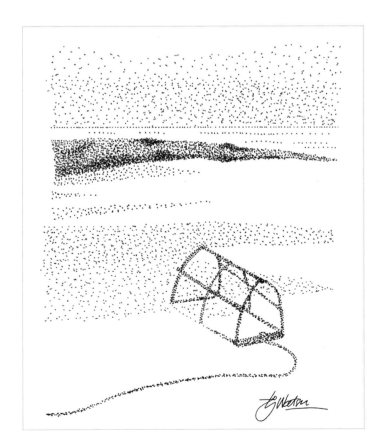

Both images:
Tez Watson
Black & white/
Pen & Ink
2480 x 3508 px

New York Dialogue

Every fall, Ruby-throated Hummingbirds visit Central Park on migration to their Mexican winter home. Their flight paths bring them into contact with the local grey squirrels (ardillas)*. With luck, you may hear them conversing.*

Hey, Ruby, you seen my nuts?
You talkin to me, Ardilla?
Yeah, you up there wid da ruby throat.
You no see I am occupado?

What ya doin, boid?
I'm afuellin op, estupido!
Hey watch wid da beak!
I no get time for this.

So what's da hurry?
What the horry?
Yeah, what's da big rush?
You never migrated?

No, I never needed to. I got my nuts.
You jost say you loss them.
I'm always losin em - ya never lost nothin?
No, jost I must find the flores with the good nectar.

So where's yer wings Ruby, I don't see em?
You no see them because they too fast for you!
Hey boid, ya got some beak!
Si ratoncito, an it's goin right in this blue Salvia.

Wow, you sure can drink Ruby.
You better believe it Ardilla, I no got choice.
So where ya headed?
South, follow the sun, follow the flores.

OK boid, I like yer style - I'm gonna help ya.
Como? How you goin to help me?
You scratch my fur, I scratch yer feathers.
No entiendo, Ardilla.

Blue Salvia - they gotta big patch south of the reservoir.
That is good ratoncito.
So, what about my nuts?
Two steps to the front, five to the left.

Hey, Ruby, ya hit the spot!
You sure about them Salvias?
Sure as acorns is acorns!

Martin Walsh

Broadford Works I.

Katarina Chomova
Colour / mixed media
2D 1360 x 1200 mm

Threips

It's the last train fae Innercant tae Meikle Girnie an it seems tae Fergus Gowkie he's the ainlie bodie on the train; that alane, he wunners gin thare's e'en a driver. Meikle is the terminus for the line nouadays, for the bit haudit tae Little Girnie an yont is closed this fiftie year bygane lik, sae thare's naebodie gaun ithergaits nou thare's ainlie the Meikle stap left. Fergus is veisitin his auld fere Douglas an aince aff o the train maun walk the twa kilometre tae whar he bides i Little.

The train begins slawin tae it's creepin alang, an a disembodied vyce lats ken it's winnin tae Meikle. As Fergus leuks ower the windae, the kenspeckle sicht o Meikle station kythes tae'm. While the train snuves intae the station afore stellin at the hinneren, he sees the place is as desert o fowk as the train. It aye his a gowstie an oorielik sense tae'm, but maistlie whan this quate an late at een. Lik mony a station o a burgh o sic a size, it's been a hantle mair thrang, but wi the motor vehicle displacin the train, muckle o't forleit an negleckit syne, an that wey helpin giein it the cast it his tae Fergus.

Thare's ainlie the ae pletform uised at Meikle nou it's but a brainch line, an for ornar ainlie the ae train at the station - or nane - for the train fae Innercant tae Meikle becomes the train fae Meikle tae Innercant. Fergus is gey surpreesed, syne, tae see anither train, an sittin ower at an auld pletform i the pairt o the station nae langer uised. Wi thare bein nae chase for him gittin aff o his ain train, an unco curious, he his a guid leuk tae the meisterie ane. He sees it's an auld warld thing – an fowk abuird it! Nou he's keen o a closer leuk tae this ferlie sae hoys aff o the train.

The uised an forleit pairts o the station is sindert wi a fit brig that's mou Fergus's side o't is steikit wi a hie metal fence. He gaes up tae the fence, disjaskit wi time an negleck, an throu a slap in it. As he sterts ower the brig, he turns a tait thochtit forbye curious for whit he micht fin, or be row'd intae even, sae slaws doun some an caas cannie while free tae win aff fae the sain belyve - tho he disna richt ken whit it is he's feart for.

Aince oot ower the brig, houaniver, he leuks tae the train, sees twa-three o the passengers wag him ower tae thaim, an this wey encouraged forrit loses mynd o onie thocht. Whan he gits tae thaim he sees the train is stow'd wi sodgers, an aa in an auld-farrant uniform lik the ane his gransher wure i the photies o'm i the Gret Weir.

Ane o the sodgers that waggit him greets him.

"Guid een sin. We hae been here this twa our an nae tint nor trial o muvin. Can ye see the driver, or some ither bodie wirks here, an mebbie git wit whan we'll be leain an lat us ken? We canna git oot wir charrit an thare's nae staff here aboot for us tae speir at."

Whit a wey tae sair sodgers, Fergus thinks, myndin his ain gransher left this verra place for the Waster Front i 1915. He is positive tae help thaim as thai askit.

"Ay, A'll can dae that."

"That's awfu guid o ye sin", the sodger replies, an Fergus sets awa.

Firstlins he gaes tae the front o the train for tae see the driver. He passes charrits ane efter ither thrang o sodgers. Whan he gits tae the ingin thare's naebodie thare.

Syne he returns ower the fit brig tae the pairt o the station uised nouadays. He kens the bodie tae see nou is the station agent Tam McKendrick - he can see nae ither bodie aboot onieweys. He's the brither tae Alan McKendrick that's an umwhile Professor o Fergus's at the Universitie he hid three-fower muckle threips wi anent his lairnin. The brithers can be the same for houtin, an bein natterie an snotterie at, fowk thai thraw wi – thare's no ane o thaim tae mend the ither – but he's the bodie tae see for aa.

Fergus kens whar McKendrick wull be on a cauld nicht lik this: in his wee office gittin a heat an wi a het drink aboot haun. He gangs up tae the office door an chaps on it.

"C'wa ben", a vyce cries.

He apens the door an deed McKendrick is sittin forenent a wee electric lowe wi a drink narhaun on his dask. He's leukin tae Fergus while still haudin apen the copie o the *Speirar* he's readin.

"Ay, whit can A dae for ye?"

"The fowk on the train yont the fit brig is wantin tae ken whan thai'r leain the station."

"Whit fowk, whit train?"

"Lik A say'd, the fowk on the train yont the fit brig."

"Thare's nae train thare; hisna been for years."

"Ay thare is. A wis on the Innercant train an saw it whan we got in the station. An A've been ower tae it an talkit wi a bodie on it."

"Thare's nae sic train. Awa wi ye an dinna be at me wi yer haivers."

"Wull ye no tak tent tae whit A'm sayin. Thare's a train yont the fit brig an the fowk on it is wantin tae ken whan thai'r leain."

"Thare isna a train thare! Think ye A dinna ken whit's whit here an me the station agent? Nou awa wi ye!"

A thocht comes tae Fergus that he turns an leuks ower the lane smaa windae. Ay! The sodgers' train canna be seen fae the office, for at the verra least it's dern'd wi the train he cam in, an that gies 'im the owerhaun.

"Ye canna see it fae here, for the Innercant train's i the gate an that," he says tae McKendrick while still an on leukin ower the windae, an than turns again tae speak face for face, "c'wa ower the fit brig an see it for yersel."

McKendrick kens thare's nae train ower the fit brig, but nou feels it maun be proven wi Fergus's challenge - an the easiest an suinest wey o bein shot o'm onieweys. Forbye, Fergus's mainer is that aefauld seemin, he's begun misdootin his ain sel a wee.

"Richt than, lat's see," he annunces as he closes his paper an gets up. He draps the paper on tae the dask an stramps oot the office wi Fergus follaein him.

The twasum gaes up tae an throu the slap i the fence that steiks the mou o the fit brig an oot ower the brig itsel. Aince ower, thai hae a scance o the hail o the auld station nou forleit.

"See, thare's nae train thare, no the stime o ane", declares McKendrick triumphantlie.

"Weel it's gaen nou", says Fergus, "whitten a station agent ir ye? Ye dinna ken a train's come, ye dinna ken a train's here, ye dinna ken a train's awa. A'm awa masel, awa hame."

An he wis.

The En

Hamish Scott

Flip

Mark Regester
Colour/digital photography
2400 x 1291px

Talpidae Have Twelve Fingers

If I were a mole
shuddering earth before me
like the bombs that drop on the city do
I would burrow deep, Australia-deep
where there are no bombs
no spare limbs unaccounted for.

Mum - why did Mrs Granger have three legs?
and she pushed me onto the next train so it seemed –
I don't see or hear bombs drop now.

Instead, I sit at the field edge
watch moles hanging motionless on barbed wire
while Granddad tells me tales from the other war
ignoring pleas to *hush up now, Bill*
(from Grandma).

Tales of mole-men
tunnelling
listening
listening.

He said they didn't need eyes
and in my dreams
I see their blood-black sockets
their extra limbs
their mole hands
gouging at the earth.

Helena Sanderson

About The Weather

She's a drizzle of a figure, digging
in a downpour, storm-shambled,
rooted in a rainpool.

There's a pane between them, misting
with his breathing. She's adrift
from him now, he's watching her sinking.

They've had words about her behaviour,
soft sounds spoken into the brittle air.
Still, she's out there.

She is coaxing the bright, the living,
with all her care. He won't ask again,
he knows it's health itself she's tending.

She had words with the surgeons
those fierce weeks he found her
in a morphine stupor.

The operation haunts her, years after.
And the anguish he learned of later
in the blood-well of their sheets

was a sorrow planted in their garden.
She is digging from memory now,
searching for seeds

among the rocks and heather.
She knows everything
about the weather.

Eddie Gibbons

Cold, Dark and Deep

Julie-Ann Simpson
Colour / Oil on paper
2D 610 x 450 mm

Oscar's Ladder

The windows shatter and a warm breeze enters, lifting a foul smell and the dog lifts its head and many of the single men in the lakeside shacks wake from their slumber and lift their heads, too, peering out of their broken windows, looking down the line to see others looking back at them or forward across the lake, up to the sun that sits in the centre. Some retreat back into their rooms. Some come out onto the wooden decking and start picking up the broken glass. A few just come out and sit in their armchairs, smoking, drinking a bottle of beer or a glass of rum, holding their hands to their heads or fingers quizzically to their chins, staring slightly upwards to the large white question marks forming from the top of their heads before they float up to join the other small clouds in the sky.

A few of the dogs run out of the open doors and begin playing with each other on the pockets of sand and grass lining the water. Some fucking. Some fighting. Many others remain in the men's shacks, curiously sniffing the broken glass, the edge of the door. Some sleep on after checking if the noise brought food, each damp nose nested neatly back, each paw limp again.

One man walks out onto his decking, feeling fatigue and a slight hangover. His shorts are a little scruffy and his socks and boots are off. This man's dog hasn't stirred. It hasn't checked for food. It hasn't yet smelt the foul smell. The man sits in his armchair and looks left and right, then he looks at the shack immediately to his right and begins to circle the lake, looking for any peculiar detail in each shack that his eyes pass. All he sees are men in shorts, some in jeans, some naked, walking to and from their decking, checking their windows, smoking their cigarettes. Large clouds have begun to form above the lake due to the confusion and the sand is losing the light, becoming grey. The sun sits above the dark mass and begins to raise up, higher and higher into the sky. Droplets of rain begin to fall and the dogs are called in with names like Boomer, Musket, C.J, Mister.

This man's dog is named Rodney. This man is named Oscar. Oscar sits on his chair as the rain falls and tat-tats on the thin metal roofing. It is warm, maybe the beginning of a summer. He pulls out a Blue Vine cigarette and chinks open his lighter. Flame. Inhale. The foul smell has faded. The smell of damp salt warm and wool has begun. He is now wearing his thick grey jumper, some dark green hiking socks finishing a little higher on his shins than his worn black boots. Comfort, as he rests his feet up on a wooden stool opposite his chair and chuffs his Blue Vine whilst pouring a small glass of rum from the bottle by the door. Ice clinks and one of Rodney's ears raise, a little lazily. He exhales a heavy breath and then returns to his boring dreams.

"Fucking pointless, isn't it, eh? Fucking pointless. Listen, champ, if you were to give me a handfulla... " Oscar sits in silence. The occasional moan from a neighbour can be heard further down the way. The tat-tats of raindrops and the odd call loses its fear across the water and falls to weakness: Boome... Musket... C.J... Mister...

"Musket?! Musket?!" calls Neighbour from Shack to Oscar's Left. "What seems to be the matter there, Neighbour? Lost your pooch?" "Musket? Musket?!" "Maybe he went for a swim, eh?! Maybe he was sick of the sight of ya and went for a long swim in the lake!" Oscar dumps his cigarette onto the wood decking and rubs it out with the tip of a boot. "Musket?! Musket?!" "Or maybe he's in here! Hiding away with Rodney! Hey, Musket, you in here ol' pal? Hiding away from Neighbour are ya? Touches you does he?! He does?! Oit, Neighbour! Ol' Musket here says you've been touching him! Is that true?!" "Musket? Musket?!" "Oit, Neighbour! I'm talking to you! You should be taken off the lake, chap!

You should be put away, mate!" "Musket?! Musket?!" Oscar swirls the ice in his glass and lights another cigarette. "Nah... I was only fucking around. I haven't got ya dog in here. Just Rodney. Me and Rodney. Rodney and I, as they say, eh!"

Neighbour silences, turns and walks directly back into his shack, the door leaning closed behind him. "Yeah, just Rodney and meself, sitting in the shack, thinking what to do, dar de dar de dar, loo be do be do... Rodney, you still there, chief?" Rodney stretches, pushing small soft mounds of air to the side with his two front paws. Dog yawn. Stand up shake and he walks slowly outside. "Hello, chap. Mind the food in your bowl, bud, you don't want it going stale left out there all the time. Eat up." And Rodney obliges. Nom, nom. "Good lad. I love you, buddy. What are we going to do today, eh? Say, how's about we see how many bottles of rum I can get through before being stupid enough to jump in the lake, eh? You can join me, as ever, young brute, but no cigarettes for you this time. How does that sound?" Rodney, listening to Oscar's thoughts, keeping ninety-nine percent of his attention to his food, lifts his hairy head and turns it to make eye contact without moving his body. "You've got a fuckin' deal there, Oscar, me old boy." "Good boy! Alright, let's get cracking..."

Oscar and Rodney sat that day out, on the decking, sipping back rums and ice at a leisurely pace until they'd emptied four bottles of dark liquor into glass and bowl and laughed over many fictitious stories together.

"The sun crept over us in the morning hours and held the Earth, etc." "The waves were glittered by the new day sun, etc." "The room was filled with an early November sun, etc." "Faces were bleached by the sun, heating their cheeks against the winter wind, etc." "As the sun sat eleven am high, the Earth kept turning, moving closer to the sun, etc." "The sun, etc." "The sun hung there looking toward the depth of its fall, etc." "The beaks of birds were filled with small limbs due to the help from the sun, etc." "Photo-fucking-synthesis was made possible by the old June sun and the plants held their hands up in peace signs, rocking their heads to heavy drums and psychedelic guitars ... and sun. The plants went, 'fucking yeah, bro. Gimme sol!' Etc." "The sun smiles on those who hold their hands to it, etc." "The sun brings warmth and safety and growth, etc." "The sun's fucking *great*, etc." "Oscar, believe me, the sun and I - *aahhhhh*," (Rodney chewing and licking at his underbelly) "I knew this one s - *ahhhhh*," (and again) "Sorry. So this sun..." "Tell me, Rodney." Etcetera...

They sat and lied to each other for hours on end, Oscar talking about great men doing great things then Rodney would respond with a story of an even greater dog doing even greater things. Oscar would tell him of presidents and war heroes and Rodney would tell him of huge packs of wolves trailing continents and dogs that had built entire cities unknown to man. Occasionally they would look at each other, laugh under their lowered eyelids and pop open another bottle, saluting the lake. Oscar would fill up Rodney's bowl and Rodney would drag out another pack of ice from the bucket in the shack.

On days like this, they would sometimes tell each other tales of such magnitude that not only did they disbelieve each one that was shared, they also argued and debated about the realistic probabilities that these stories *could* actually occur. During the night as their arguments would grow into bitter tongues and their guts became ravaged by booze, Oscar would stand and launch empty bottles in all directions, displaying his anger and each time, once the bottles flew, they would both quickly retire back to the shack so as not to be blamed. The sun would slowly fall from its suspended spot, a star at first, slowly growing bigger and brighter, rounder and hotter before stopping above the lake, its heat clearing the clouds and drying the rain and shining on the confused faces of men peering out of their broken windows.

Days and weeks and years pass like this and always have. Some days spent in silence, looking out over the wide round lake, up to the central sun through the dainty clouds before they became thick and wet and the sun retired high. Some days would be spent telling stories and ending in arguments and bottles flown. Some would be spent walking around the lake, looking at Neighbours and the Other Dogs and whispering whether or not they prefer them to the ones shacked up in Shack to Oscar's Left or Shack to Oscar's Right. Their appearance never changes. The world turns around the lake and all is as it should and will never cease to be.

~~~

The window shatters and a warm breeze enters, lifting a foul smell and Rodney lifts his head and many of the single men in the lakeside shacks wake from their slumber and lift their heads, too, peering out of their broken windows, looking down the line to see others looking back at them or forward across the lake, up to the sun that sits in the centre. Rodney sighs and looks along the wooden flooring up to the door, beneath and past the bed to see if Oscar is up and standing, too lazy to lift his head against the gravity. Raising both eyes he sees some toes hanging out from the covers. "Wake the fuck up, man. Come on…" They both groan and their breath stains. Oscar remembers throwing up out on the decking the night before.

Movement occurs on the bed. Oscar scratches his arse intensely for a few long seconds before quickly sniffing his hand and pulling the blankets back over him. "Oscar, did you chuck up out there? That stinks, man…" "*Eeearrgghhh*… Yea… Sorry, buddy. I'll get to it…just…my eyes sting bad, eh. Giv'us a minute."

Rodney tries to go back to sleep but the smell is too strong and his eyes open once again to scan the floor. By the base of the broken window lays an empty bottle. "Fuckers…" Oscar grunts from under his blanket. "What's that?" "These fuckers, in my dream, man… Took all the, er… Ah, shit. I don't really remember." "Hey, Oscar…" "What's up, champ?" Rodney notices a small roll of white paper in the bottle on the floor. "Oscar, we've got mail, mate." "Oh, yea? Who's that from then?" This has never happened before and Oscar almost sweats stress as he tries to think of a witty continuation to rhetoric.

"There's some paper in the bottle." "What bottle?" "*What bottle?! The* bottle. There's a bit of paper inside it." Oscar's toes quickly disappear underneath the cover and his back arches up against the back wall of the shack. He looks down beneath the window. Rodney's back becomes visible from beside the bed and he looks up and over to Oscar. Oscar looks to Rodney. Oscar looks to the bottle. Rodney walks to the foot of the bed and looks to the bottle.

Dear Oscar & Rodney,

It is my greatest pleasure to inform you that you have been selected for Day Out.

Good luck and congratulations.

Sincerely,

Message In A Bottle

~~~

I told you I wanna fuck in the movies! It doesn't quite work like that, Ms. Arnold. I got prettier tits and a tighter ass than any broad I ever seen on the fuckin' box! Go on, gimme a part in a movie! No, Ms. Arnold. Now would you please leave... Fuck you! Hey, er...guys, what, er... what's the problem here? She's the best in the business. I'm sorry, who are you? I'm Harry. Never mind him! You know, I've acted before! OH, YES! I done a lot! Ah, forget these fucks! Come on, Harry! Er...sure thing, baby. You guys are fuckin' liars, ya hear?! Thank you, Ms. Arnold... Harry.

The white door swings open and Ms. Arnold comes storming out followed tentatively by Harry Fewteeth. She looks to Rodney. "Auw! What a cute lil puppy, right?! Harry! Would you look at how cute this lil puppy is!" "It's real cute, baby." Rodney looks up to her. "Auw, he's adorable! I wanna pooch like that! Is he yours, mister? What's his name?" "His name's Rodney." "Hey, Rodney. How you doin' lil guy?" Harry on one knee. "Leave 'im alone, Harry! He don't want you he wants me! Look at 'im! He's looking right at me! Is he yours, mister?" "Yea, he's my friend." Harry looks up to Oscar. "Dogs a man's best friend, right?" "Right..."

Ms. Arnold and Harry stand side by side for a quiet second looking down at Rodney. They then look up to Oscar, smile, and saunter off down the white hallway cursing those they were speaking to in the room.

"Next please..." Rodney looks to Oscar who is sitting on a white chair beside the white door. "Ok, chap. That's us." "You got it, Rodney."

The room is white and all inside is white, too. On the far wall opposite the door are two large windows allowing a lot of sunlight to enter the room. In front of this is a large white desk, two chairs in front, empty, and two chairs behind with one black woman and one black man in white suits sitting on them. Many white papers without words are covering the desk in neat piles. Some clipped together. Some in white folders. A white cigarette burns away as it sits in a white ashtray beside the woman's arms folded on the table on which she rests her head. The woman's head raises and the pair speak in unison. "Ah, welcome! Oscar and Rodney, right?" "That's us. I'm Oscar. He's Rodney." "Oh! What a beautiful dog! Does he do any tricks?" Rodney jumps up onto one of the empty chairs opposite those in white. "Fucking woof." "OH! Beautiful! Just fantastic!" Rodney fucking woofs and woofs some more. "EXCELLENT! MARVELLOUS!" Oscar sits in the other chair beside Rodney. "We received a message, the 'Message In A Bottle.' "Lovely touch, don't you think?" Rodney nods, looks to Oscar. Oscar nods.

"So, why are we here? What's this day out all about?" Rodney turns back to the pair in white and questions, "Who are you two?" The woman opens a small white drawer in the desk and removes two small nametags. She places one above her left breast and slides the other, slowly, along the table to the man. The woman's name is Beatrice. The man slowly picks up the badge and pins it above his left breast. The man's name is Bernard, emphasis on the *ar*. Beatrice and Bern*ar*d look at each other, nod, and then look back to Oscar and Rodney. "Right...so, "Oscar squints at their name tags through all the light and white, "Beatrice and Bernard." "That's Bern*aarr*d, emphasis on the *a* and the *r*." "Got ya. Beatrice and Bern*aarr*d. What's this 'day out' mentioned in the bottle?" "Well, guys, you've been selected from the other blanks for a day out." "Where to?" Rodney and Oscar question. "You'll be travelling to the lake!" "What lake?" They question further. "The one you've just come from, silly!" Rodney looks to Oscar in confusion. Oscar looks to Rodney. They both look back to those in white.

Samuel A Verdin

The Alternative Tourist Tour of Properties Owned by Nyaffs

In Aiberdeen takk a turn roon a seaside High Rise
Check oot the guff o pee in the lift, the brukken intercom
The graffiti scrawled ower the waas on the secunt storey
Fur the ultimate frisson (by-passin the stank o fish comin aff the sea)
Step ower the druggies jackin up on the stairs
Dinna pet the pit bull on the landin
Its teeth are mingin.   Its temper's legendary

In Dundee, veesit anither colourful schemie
Step throw the yett o flat nummer thirtythree
The guide weirs leopard skin tights
Is perma-tanned like an orange
She luiks like a chanty-rassler on a spree
Dinna feed her fartin cat
It'll gie ye flechs an gob on ye
Makk sure yer inoculatit fur dysentry

Embro's sublet aff frae a close is a must
Takk tent o the gairden's lanscapin
The rippit sofa stukken wi gaffa tape
Luik on the scene wi envy, Mr Paul Getty
The brukken Ikea press, mangst the nettles an dug keech
The peelin plaster gnomes, an the terracotta warrior
Minus twa airms like the Venus de Milo
Chappt aff bi a minger wallopin a machete

In Glesgae, step inno an up-mairket semi-detached
The guide here, Fat Shuggy, is modelling his favourite gear
A mankini aneth a peenie wi plastic boobs
Based o the paps o ane o thon Hollywid stars
Check oot the thatch o his chest hair
Ye cud beery Govan in it
His bling can be seen frae Mars

Inverness features a bijou but–n-ben
Fur European wirkers.   Nine o them share a bed
In shifts o three. The bath has twinty nine tidemerks
The loo boasts a crinoline dallie ower the lavvie roll
There's an Elvis Presley lampstaun wintin a shade
The ashtray is reamin wi tabbies. The carpet's clarty
Like yer waukin on superglue. The doorbell chimes 'Amarillo'
Jist for you. Midgies makk up the protein in the soup
The plastic flooers in the windae hae brewer's droop

Sheena Blackhall

Queen Victoria Visits a Medium

One night they came 'round our hoose,
tore a strip off Ma's vest an
packed Uncle Jackie's cheeks
till his accent changed.

Aunty Annie demanded a shilling
an silence.   No rustling
petticoats or crinkling brow
to flicker the candle flame.

An Mrs Brown, all regal-like
on stiff-backed chair, waited
for a glimpse of her Albert
or an 'I love you' wheezed
through wet muslin.

Lynda Nash

Shoreline

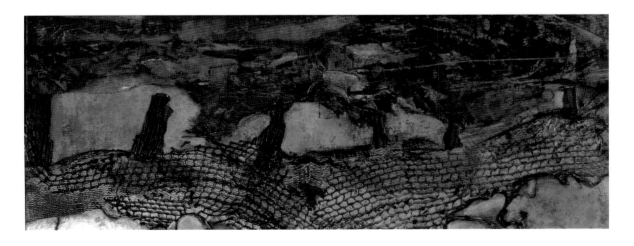

Rosemary Bassett
Colour / Collograph, Collage and Acrylic
2D 456 x 171 mm

Mugwort

Katarina Chomova
Colour / mixed media
2D 900 x 900 mm

Water Colours

Patricia squeezes her fingers together and points her toes as she slices through the water. Her dive propels her way out in front of the other girls. She swims like a seal – silken and sleek, hardly a splash from her feet. Her tumble turn is a full two meters before the others and resembles a pirouette more than a twist and push. From the poolside come shouts of encouragement as she nears the finish and then eruptive whoops as she touches the wall. She blinks back her goggles and looks for her dad in the stalls. He's on the phone but giving her the thumbs up. She's through to the final.

"Good work Patricia," says the coach Mr McGuiness patting her pink swimming cap. "You're through to the final."

She pulls herself out of the pool and tucks her forefingers under and along the back hem of her costume, snapping the elastic back in place. Over the last year Patricia has become increasingly aware of her swimming costume. She has always been tall for her age but now bumps were starting to grow and she was secretly borrowing her father's razor. She tried to argue with Mr McGuiness that the gala costumes were too high at the thigh but apparently they were 'regulation.' She didn't want to give up swimming.

Patricia has always worked hard at improving her strokes. A natural talent. 'My little goldfish,' her mother had called her. Even when she was little she would swim three lengths to Mum's one. She could still see her doing the breaststroke, gliding through the water, holding her head high to keep her hair dry and avoid getting water in her eyes. When young, Patricia could see perfectly below the surface and would watch the bend of people's bodies in the light. She often wondered how light refracted. Mum would hold a glass brim full of water to sunlight and Patricia would catch the reflection on white card. She had all the colours of the rainbow displayed in a semi-circle – sitting in the palm of her hand. To Patricia it was as if water could contain all the colours of the world. She would imagine her warm body acted like a prism as she swam around, casting rainbows of light around the universe.

Craig moves down two rows of stalls and sits next to her. Translucent crystal droplets of water hang on his body shining in the bright competition light. Under the towel, Patricia's skin bristles like soft whiskers to be so near to him. Craig is the regional champion. He sits feet planted firmly, elbows on knees wearing nothing but Speedos and flip-flops whilst other swimmers cower under extra large t-shirts. She notices his tanned wrists, the smooth, powerful bone curving into the hand. She turns away, her stomach tumbling, then focuses on unfurling her hair from her cap. The elastic tugs at her scalp, squeaking through her fingers. She used coconut shampoo this morning and hopes she might overcome the pungent smell of chlorine.

"Was that your PB?" asks Craig.

"I didn't see the time," she says without looking at him. "Mr McGuiness'll tell me later."

She faces the pool, eyes glazed. Craig nods and looks out across the pool trying to see what she's staring at. The under-tens are ready for their freestyle relay, their tiny bodies bobbing up and down, ready to race. Patricia takes the opportunity to look over her shoulder at her dad. He's typing something on a laptop with one hand and talking on the phone with the other. A twitchy swimming attendant points to a sign showing a camera barred with a red line.

"It's not a camera," he mouths.

The attendant walks round the pool and takes the steps two by two. He whispers in his ear asking if there is a photo function to the device. Patricia's dad nods reluctantly. He gets up, gathers bits of paper, snaps his laptop shut and pats his pockets for keys and loose change. He always looks as though he's lost something, thinks Patricia. She returns his wave as her dad goes outside.

"Lane two, that's my little sister," says Craig pointing at a girl in a purple swimming costume.

Patricia cranes her neck. "I didn't realise you had a sister at the club."

"Yeah, Natalie." Craig tightens his lips. "She's such a pain. She just won't leave me alone. She's always like, *give me that, it's mine!*" He whines and thrusts out his chest, shimming as he says it.

Patricia smiles at him.

"You got any brothers or sisters?"

Patricia shakes her head. "Just me and Dad," she says. She feels an urge to tell Craig that he should feel lucky to have a sister. He has a family – a full family. She remembers how her mother taught her to swim. She wants to describe her smiling face with wet, slicked black hair, her arms windmilling in the air to demonstrate front crawl. But Patricia realises now she is scared: the memory is beginning to fade. That mostly what she remembers is Mum's closeness, wrapping her arms beneath her, supporting her in the water, her fingers spread under the belly as she learned to float. Sometimes she steals into Mum's wardrobe and smells her clothes, but the perfume has long since gone.

The whistle goes and Natalie squats holding her hands together in a long V above her head. There is no push from her legs and she simply belly-flops into the pool. Plop!

Craig purses his lips sucking in a hiss through his teeth. "See you later," he says and goes to warm up for his race. Patricia tries to smile but after he is gone realises she has been frowning.

To acclimatise his skin to the temperature, Craig folds into the water slowly. He rolls his shoulders round in circles and flexes his arms behind him before dipping his head under. He blows out a measured stream of bubbles to the surface, then, grasps the two silver handles at the side of the starter block and pulls himself, chin up, to the wall. He is a tight ball, a coiled spring. Patricia can see the veins in his arms stand out, pulsing paths for his blood as it accelerates through his body. He is ready.

Watching Craig is a master class. The whistle goes and the swimmers arch back undulating in the water. He creates the biggest ripples, with a rhythmic slapping of his arms as he reaches back with every stroke. Water dips in to accommodate his body as if his navel has created a new centre of gravity. Patricia notices the final beam in the ceiling he will use as a marker for the end of the pool and, like clockwork, he pulls his leading arm into his body, tucks his chin into his chest and rotates. He brings his legs up towards his chest to form a perfect tuck; head in, knees in, feet in. Push. He butterfly-kicks a full four meters below the surface, undulating like an electric eel before breaking through with the heave of his hand. He ploughs through the water, Mr McGuiness pacing with him the length of the pool, getting faster and faster. Craig flippers through the water pulling his body backwards as if he has two rotary blades fitted at his shoulders. "Go, go, go..." chant the stalls getting louder and louder towards the edge of the pool. His arm thwacks off the side and he scrapes his hand off the rough surface. He's won.

Patricia wraps her towel more tightly round her shoulders and goes to the bathroom to get away from the noise. As she passes Craig, she notices he holds his arm out of the water. Small scratches squeeze beads of blood. She winces, tight in her stomach, and feels the hard pattern of the floor beneath her feet. In the bathroom Patricia waits for a cubicle. She is careful not to touch anything and stands, arms folded over her towel, over her breasts. She can tell the room has been recently hosed as water drips from the bottom of the white sinks and the smell of freshly applied bleach fingers her nose. A cubicle comes free. To Patricia, her limbs feel over-stretched, elongated and awkward. Bloated almost. She splays her toes on the toilet floor and feels her belly. It is slightly misshapen, a heavy sponge. Maybe it is the light, she reasons, until she goes to flush. In the bowl there is a red flash, a crimson fish floating on the white. It blinks at her. Patricia stares at it. She strokes her soft belly and stares again. Sure enough, on a second tissue she finds a wet trace, crimson and glossy. She flushes and watches the streaks tumble and twist away as if they were alive. *Not now,* she pulses to herself. A thought grabs her and she twists her towel round searching through the pattern for signs. Sure enough there is one tiny spot diluted by the pool water where she has sat. It is faint but it is there. A blot of blood as acid as a battery. Her friends have talked about it at school – how it feels, even the taste. Like iron says one. Like curdled milk says another. But most of all they have talked about it at home. They've been explained to, how it all works. Down there. Inside.

Patricia has one thought. *Leave.* It is a prayer in her head, a panic on her lips. Through the door she spies her bag - the far end of the galley, leaning against a stall. Her father is back, checking his watch, legs crossed. He doesn't see her. She breaths in and glues her eyes to the floor.

"There she is," points Craig, and Mr McGuiness grabs her by the shoulders.

"We've been looking for you everywhere," he snaps. She can feel his soft hands on her skin, his thumb a hairsbreadth away from the nape of her neck.

"I can't," she pleads, but Mr McGuiness pushes her to lane four.

"Do your best," he says, stopwatch ready.

On the starting block she imagines red droplets running rivers down her, pooling at her feet, between her toes. She steps down and twists her hair up into her orange cap pulling it tight to her temples. She bends down on the pretence of flicking water over her arms and chest but checking for any droplets. She stays there, squatting, hiding herself beside the starting block. She rinses each eye of her goggles and wipes the mist forming from the inside with her fingers. Nothing is showing but to Patricia it is only a matter of time. She spies Mr McGuiness flapping at her, ushering her to the platform from the side of the pool. She steps onto the block and concentrates.

The whistle sounds. From the moment Patricia hits the water, she is conscious of everything she does. Her arms slap the viscous liquid. One, two, three. Turn the head. Breathe. Nine leg beats. Three to each stroke.

"Kick from the hip," Mr McGuiness yells from the side. She points her toes, flippering the water away. She sees the wall ahead and prepares herself for the turn but this change in rhythm makes her falter. She fears a red trail behind her. Blooming jewels glistening in the water. All eyes on her. Lead arm up and tumble forward. She feels her skin prickle as she pushes off the wall. She glides but neglects her butterfly kick - a full wave of the body to propel her to victory but her heavy sponge-like tummy pulls her straight. She finishes the length and the gala claps her politely in last place.

She waits until the commotion has died down and sinks below the buoys towards the ladder. Hurriedly, she gathers up her stuff and returns to the bathroom. In the mirror above the sink, she sees her sockets are still ringed from the suction of her goggles. Her eyes bulging. Popping out. Her whole body – popping out. Patricia the manatee. Patricia the whale. A cubicle lock cracks to green, opens and Natalie comes through. She doesn't stop at the sink. Instead, she bounces her bum off the door and her slim body goes directly through to the pool. Patricia quickly locks the cubicle door. She rolls the cheap tissue paper around and around her fist, stuffs it in her knickers and pulls them up. She is careful not to drag her jeans on the floor and buttons them carefully at the waist. Walking to the car she can hear the tissue crushing between her legs with every step she takes. It's a faint rustling like leaves in the trees. Craig is talking to the winner. A toothy-grin. His fingers brush the girl's arm. Patricia bends her head, pretending to fiddle with the strap of her rucksack. She climbs in the back of Dad's tatty Volvo.

"You were great out there," he says.

She pulls on her seatbelt and sinks a little in the foamy seat. She wonders if she should mention it to her father or not. What would he care?

He looks at her in the rear-view mirror, sitting quiet in the back seat. "Cheer up Patty. You did really well."

"How would you know?" mumbles Patricia.

"What was that?"

"You were hardly there. You don't know. You don't know anything." The words pour out of her before she realises what she is saying. She feels the regret in her body as she's saying it.

He is quiet. He grips the wheel and turns into the roundabout.

What would Mum say, what would Mum say? thinks Patricia and rubs her red eyes with her knuckles.

Pascale Free

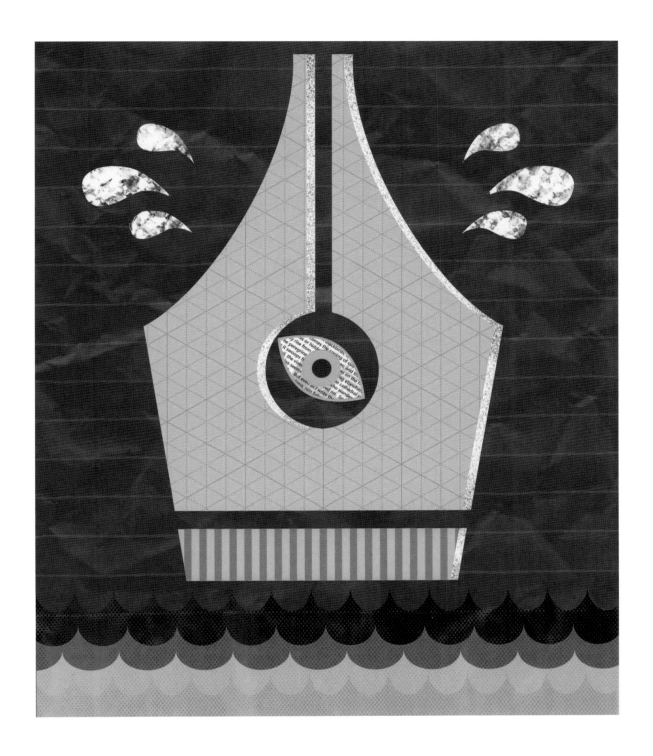

Monika Stachowiak
Colllage/Digital Media
2740 x 2790 px

A tiny bit of eczema

My mum says
I have a tiny bit of eczema.

I can't read.
I can't spell.
I'm good at thinking ideas.
And I can say things to the class.
But I can't really read or spell.
I have a tiny bit of eczema.

The sounds jump about.
They splash on the page,
landing in different places.
So words don't stay the same.
They come and go,
like the sea,
         as
           ese
             esa
               ase
                 sed
                   dse.

I can't read.
I can't spell.
I'm good at speaking my stories,
and working out how.
But I can't read or spell,
not really.

I have a tiny bit of eczema,
my mum says.

What's eczema?

Susan Miller

Santa Was Assassinated

The authorities covered it up.
Quietly, no fuss.
Parents were told to pretend.

See how awkward they seem when you ask,
What did Santa do in the Summer?

Mum will answer,
Ask your Dad, Ask your Dad.
She normally says, *Ignore what he says.*

Or if you ask, *Who delivered presents*
when Santa was a boy?
Dad will mumble,
Ask your Mum, Ask your Mum.

Then read his sports page;
like he sometimes does when he's listening to her.

Or they look as if they're thinking quickly.
Santa's parents delivered.
Possibly his Nan.
As if we couldn't think that up by ourselves.

Or they both give,
in the same flat sounding voice,
what sounds like a prepared answer.
Like we give when we get caught taking biscuits.

Santa makes nice presents in his grotto
all through June and July and August.

Right.

You can't catch them out. Not quite.
But it all sounds a bit shaky.
Like their bed sometimes does
when they go to bed early.

Seth Crook

Demise of the Chord Organ

The platform at Haymarket was crowded. The Aberdeen train was late, and all the benches on that side of the platform were taken. My feet ached in the stiff, half-size-too-small, junk-shop cowboy boots I had bought the previous day. On the quieter south side of the platform, I found a vacant seat among many. 'Glenrothes with Thornton' read the platform departure board. How the hell did you even say that? No wonder no-one wanted to go there. I looked down at my feet, longing to slip off the scuffed cowboy boots and pull on my comfortable, worn-out sneakers in their place. But then I would have to carry the boots and they would never fit in the suitcase.

As I stepped onto the creaking, grimy hulk that I would be stuck in all the way to Inverness, I was confronted with a solid curd of luggage. Every available flat surface was stacked high.

There was no luggage car.

I found an unreserved seat and lowered myself into it, slinging my suitcase into the overhead rack that, thankfully, it was deep enough to accept. Then I hefted the eighteen-inch cube of the Magnus 300 Chord Organ onto my knees, and balanced it, cursing the size of the case. Why didn't I play something more practical? The seat was a double. It faced backwards and, on my left, instead of a window, a lozenge of grey plastic trim curved up to meet the luggage rack.

Almost immediately, the seat that separated me from the gangway was filled by a woman in a vast cable-knit cardigan from which she took a puzzle book, a pen and a packet of crisps.

As the train pulled away, I struggled to reach the inside pocket of my fringed suede jacket, but my arm seemed to have expanded, and it wedged between the upward curve of the train wall and the Magnus 300's zippered case. Spluttering with annoyance, I tried a different tactic, driving the case of the Magnus forward and upward against the back of the seat in front with my forehead. By doing this, I was able to lift my left arm a fraction and force my hand inside the jacket to extract the printout of the email from Richard Heron, my Inverness promoter. I let the Magnus fall, and used my teeth to unfold the piece of paper.

The email was short, but it did list the address of the venue I was booked to play at. This I would give to a taxi driver at the station. Not because I intended to travel by taxi, but because I had not been able to print a streetplan off the Internet. Taxi drivers were good with directions. My phone, under favourable conditions, allowed me to make phone calls, but it did not display maps.

Perth was a busy stop. Passengers disembarked, and a little way off I identified that holy grail of the second-class rail traveller - a forward-facing double table seat with a diminutive opposite neighbour.

With the Magnus Chord Organ resting under the table, I sank back and allowed my torso to spread to its natural width of a seat-and-an-eighth. I took out Heron's email again. I had been placed third on the bill. I swore under my breath. Inverness hipsters venturing out to support 'Shivering Deforest' or 'Undercounter Envelope' might well lose interest and drift off by the time I started playing. Still worse, they might stay and chat. The tone of Heron's communication was downbeat. He had not bothered with posters because nobody did - it looked like desperation, he explained. He asked whether I had tweeted. I hadn't fucking tweeted.

Two years before I travelled this same route with a Latvian bass player, Vilis Pagrabs, and his girlfriend, Šarlote, who he told me was a singer. On stage she did nothing but knit and hold up coloured cards with untranslated statements in Latvian written in scrolly marker pen. I remember wondering whether they tried the same act back home, or if they swapped languages to preserve the mystique. We had a table together, with the fourth seat for our instruments, and somewhere around the Tay estuary Vilis took an unlabelled bottle of something strong out of his faded army holdall and passed it round. We ate all the food we had, which was ten bags of crisps and a bunch of carrots we'd got out of a supermarket bin. Šarlote, who was taller than me, and bony too, with a strange, feathery mullet that cascaded down her angular shoulders, made origami birds out of the crisp packets; and Vilis drank and drank from the bottle of whatever it was until he fell asleep on the table, his cheek flat on the Formica, drool leaking slowly from his partly open mouth. Šarlote and I kissed and I put my hand under her vest and felt and felt all the individual vertebrae from her waist up to her neck. I remember trying to count them, trying not to let my erection get too obvious. From time to time Vilis would wake up and push Šarlote back in her seat away from me, but he didn't really seem to care. I did the gig on my own that night, and it was three days before Vilis was well enough to go back on stage.

Not long after Perth, I needed to piss. I put a magazine and my suede jacket on the seat, and wobbled off down the jiggling train to find the filthy cubicle with its British Rail sign (vintage rolling stock) and its fag-burns in the off-white plastic fittings. When I came back, I couldn't find my seat. I trawled down the aisle once one way, and once the other. The wagons creaked, and the countryside passed. I still couldn't find where I had been sitting. Then I noticed the squat, black case of the Chord Organ wedged under a table. At the table sat an elderly man with a neatly trimmed white beard reading a newspaper, and next to him a woman of roughly the same age, chewing and staring into space. She was sitting in my seat.

"Hey," I said. "I think that's where I was sitting."

It wasn't a good opener, but it was the best I could think of. The old man said nothing. The woman chewed and stared into space. On each of the fingers of her left hand she wore several large, golden rings and, as she chewed, she drummed with this hand on her tan handbag, which sat perched on the table in front of her.

"I think you're in my seat," I said.

"No," said the old woman, noticing me for the first time. "The guard told us to sit here." "She blinked and chewed, and blinked again. On the tan wedge of her handbag, her fingers drummed.

"Didn't you notice I'd left my coat on the seat?" I demanded.

"Didn't notice it," said the old woman. The old man said nothing.

"Well can I have it?" I asked.

The old woman dug under her buttocks and pulled out my jacket. She handed it to me. Then she pulled out my magazine. She handed me that too.

"I have a forty-six inch chest," I said. "How could you possibly not notice it?"

The old woman chewed and gazed out of the window. The old man carried on reading his newspaper.

"You knew perfectly well it was my seat," I said, "and you sat there anyway. It's incredibly rude, and someone as old as you should know better."

The old woman chewed. The old man carried on saying nothing. I retreated down the carriage and took another seat. This one was another window seat with a table and, as far as I could see, identical to the one that had been hijacked by the old couple. If I had had any money, I would have spent it on drink from the trolley. Richard Heron had promised me a split of the door, a bag of chips and his girlfriend's sofa. 'A split of the door.' That could mean anything.

Abandoning the Magnus 300, I lay back over the two seats I had acquired. They were just as comfortable as the ones I had lost. They had the same view. They were on the same side of the train, but the whole thing brought into my mind all the other times I had backed down, when I had rolled over rather than stand up for my rights. There was the time my girlfriend Cynthia had made me get rid of half my vinyl collection; the time Victor the lazy Spanish stoner across the hall had stopped me rehearsing before midday so he could sleep; all the times my bosses in my shitty menial jobs had told me to stay longer than I was getting paid; all the promoters who'd promised me a good meal and a crate of beer, then showed up with crisps and a four pack of warm Carlsberg.

I tried to think of something calm; something soothing and copacetic, like hundreds of little Moog players drifting in coracles down a foaming waterway: the music video I had always wanted to record just for times like this. Not to sell; not to please the record label; not to get on fucking MTV - just to get me into a frame of mind where I was drifting too, playing my little imaginary Moog in my little imaginary coracle, drifting to happy waterways full of flying trout and swimming kingfishers. I got quite a long way into this water fantasy until I remembered a man in a fleamarket in Rotherham who'd sold me a Moog shell that turned out to be fake. I got it back home, took the cracked housing off my knackered old instrument, and found it didn't fit. I'd had thoughts of going to Rotherham, finding that fleamarket, or a different one, and confronting the guy, leaning on his stall and maybe overturning it and releasing all the doves and kicking the loose change about like in the New Testament. But instead I just kept it inside, and told myself that I couldn't afford the petrol to go to Rotherham and that I could sell the case at a car boot. It was before eBay took off. I never sold it.

After that, I tried to have a diverting sexual fantasy involving the trolley girl, but when she appeared I realised I'd have more luck fantasising about the trolley. There was enough of her to make two or maybe three trolley girls. How she got through the doorways between the carriages was beyond me. I ran my hand over my chest, shoving the heft of my man-boobs from side to side. Somehow it was comforting. I couldn't remember when I first started getting them. Maybe the trolley girl and I would be a well-matched couple.

I tried instead to sleep, but the seat incident kept going round and round my head. I should do something, I thought; I should stand up now and tear my shirt and roar and insist on my rights. I should tell the guard. There was no point telling the guard. Anyway, how would he get round the trolley girl?

I wrenched myself round in my seat to glare at the elderly couple. They sat, as though blameless, the man starting in on the crossword in his newspaper, and the woman clearing her throat, chewing, looking blankly at the window and at her drumming ring-laden hand on the handbag in front of her.

I turned away, crushing the magazine that lay in front of me, staring straight ahead, trying to find a new diversion from my impotent rage. In the corner of my eye, a figure began to pass. It was the old man. He moved past me, and way to the end of the carriage. The doors wheezed open and he left the carriage for the next one. I turned back and saw that he had left a bulging, navy blue rucksack on the seat. I suppose he thought this was going to be a good way to keep his seat until he came back. I ground the magazine a little more. By rights, the old man had not taken my seat - only the one-eighth of a seat that I had been spilling over into. On the other hand, he had said nothing when his wife had produced my jacket: positive proof that the two of them had just sat right down and stolen my place in the full knowledge of what they were doing. Silver-haired fuckers! Seat-stealing zombies with bus passes and shopping bags full of food for the cat!

On the table in front of the old man's bag was a cup of coffee. It was the sort of coffee you could only buy on a train, or from a certain type of machine in offices where the management don't care about staff turnover. It was smooth and biscuit coloured at the bottom, swelling to a fatter, ribbed section just below the rim. I could guess that inside was a scum of granules and imperfectly dissolved powdered milk that smelled like sick. I got up and walked over to the table. Then without looking at the old lady, I picked up the old man's rucksack and shoved it into the overhead rack. Then I took the cup of coffee, and, from a height of about two feet, poured it carefully and with a circular motion all over the seat. Then I put the cup down on the table and looked for a moment at the old lady. She carried on staring out of the window, drumming her fingers. She said absolutely nothing. The small middle-aged woman on the other side of the table, who had so far kept out of our dispute altogether, continued keeping out of it. She didn't say a thing. As I went back to my new seat, though, with a satisfied feeling coursing through my shoulders and chest, she took out a mobile phone and make a quiet call.

A few moments later, the old man came back. There was a babble of voices, and the old woman and the neighbour across the table explained to him what had happened to his seat, to his cup of railway coffee. I raised a finger in salute, and turned back to recline in my seat. If I had had a hat, I would have put it over my eyes. To my surprise, the old man came over and tapped me on the shoulder.

"Are you under the impression that that lady and I are travelling together?" he asked. His manner was gentle, and his tone was friendly. He was an Australian, or perhaps a Kiwi.

I said nothing.

"I have never met her before," he said. "I can understand that you're frustrated but, in the grand scheme of things, it's not very memorable. So, no need, really, to do that with the coffee." He leaned in and whispered, "To be honest, I don't think she's all there."

I stood up. "Have my seat," I said. "Have my seat and also my apologies. I'm very sorry - I was out of order."

"Made quite a bloody mess," he said, matter of factly. "I think the lady opposite called the transport police. I don't suppose they'll come out for something like this though. We're too far from a town for them to bother."

~

The platform at Carrbridge station was like main street in a western: an expanse of dusty gravel, overlooked by the whole curve of the train. I was forced out into this sodium-lit amphitheatre by the moustached guard.

"Best get off here and save any more bother, sir," he said.

"Right," I said.

I appreciated it that he had called me 'sir'. Behind him, the second-in-command, who came through the train half-hourly with a bin bag, appeared with my red cardboard suitcase and the Magnus 300 Chord Organ. The guard handed them both down. I took them and stepped back in silence. The clasps on the suitcase, which had never been sturdy, gave way, and as the train pulled off, the slipstream whipped one of my silk shirts up into the air, over the smoking diesel pipe and out of sight. I could retrieve it, I knew - there was no electric rail and the station was unmanned. In the end though, I left it. I had seen enough stage photographs of myself to know that silk showed the sweat that spread from my underarms, from my neck and from the small of my back, until the four moist areas joined up and I looked as though I had come on stage in some kind of very thin wetsuit. Some performers can hack it in knitwear, but only those at the very top of their game.

I looked in my pockets for a hat, then remembered I'd not been wearing one. I got out my phone and called Richard Heron. I felt almost good to be letting him down. Richard fucking Heron. Fuck that.

Ken Morlich

Neil Russell
Colour / Collage
2D 210 x 295 mm

Grief Walks into a Cafe

What can I get for you today?

> I don't remember who I was before the avalanche. All
> the books prepare you for the snow burial. Teach you to
> make air pockets with your hands. No one talks about the
> ice, or the rocks, or the trees. By the time they find you,
> you are frozen limbs, purple skin, branches clogging up
> your bloodstream.

Do you want any wraps or salads on the side?

> I don't know where everyone is rushing to. All I know is
> that I'm always off their tempo, but they won't let me stay,
> or leave.

Any cakes or coffee?

> There is nothing to talk about. I accidentally guzzled all
> this concrete and it is drying up inside my chest. It has
> been four hundred and ninety five days of breaths that
> turn to marble. They're prescribing me inhalers. No one's
> moved a stone.

Is that everything for you?

> Don't tell me about wells until you have licked the bottom
> – full faced and open mouthed – so many times, you
> begin to call it sweetheart.

Yani Georgieva

Border Control

I'm not sure I understand the question.
Sometimes I go home to organised chaos. There are no weather reports,
only people saying it is hot and humid. So humid,
when you scrub it off under the shower, it drips – sticky gray, like cheap spray tan.
Car horns are the national instrument.
In conversation, words roll easy off the tongue
so long as they are 'weight' and 'politics', sometimes 'electricity'.
In June I go home to salt water breeze and tomatoes the size of my head -
grandma calls them better than bread
but still offers me a slice. Like real people,
we pick green plums from the neighbourhood tree, stuff them in our shirts
and eat them barefoot on the cold concrete. My mother tongue feels foreign to people.
They make a point of asking if I'm sure it's not adopted
and yes, in autumn there are still seagulls
but bigger, more mutant - must be all that oil they guzzle. Here, home
is a makeshift tree house that has lost a roof on the bad days,
but I have built it back with two good hands.
I often ask myself - if I had to smell home,
sniff it from a row of culprits,
would I pick the Five-Spice, or the bean stew, or the granite?

Yani Georgieva

A Claustrophobic Form

Claire Cooper
Silver Gelatin Print
2D 400 x 500 mm

Tenerife

Early Sunday morn. He sweeps away the remains of the late night drinkers and smokers. Some folk might rightly call it rubbish; he see's these discarded bits and bobs as clues. Clues to what happened the night before, building stories around them - an empty beer bottle, a half eaten kebab, a lost high heel. Picturing the people who tossed these things aside, these things that meant little to them at the time, unaware that the next morning a man in his forties would be sweeping it all away and thinking about who they were, what clothes they wore and how they spoke.

It made the day pass swiftly when he thought about these ghosts from the night before. He presumed that most people had a certain disregard for what he did, not in a spiteful or condescending way he thought, just that perhaps they never spared much time to consider the nature of his work, the effort he and the rest of the lads put in. He imagined that a council street cleaner would be seen as a monotonous job by most folk. Dull, maybe even demeaning. He couldn't understand that way of thinking: not because he found it offensive or snobby - as his Auntie Marilyn would often spit "Boy's a snobby wee glaik."

That wasn't it at all; he bore no grudges against those who looked down their noses at what he did. He just couldn't understand why they would think it was dull or monotonous. Firstly it was a job: he knew plenty folk who had been on the dole most of their adult life, he was lucky to be earning, thankful even; and secondly, he got to see the city in a totally different way to most. He not only saw the remains from the night before, but through these tiny snapshots into their lives, he saw them.

They say every city has a personality, a heartbeat; well if that's true he thought, then he saw the multiple sides to that personality in his city and he certainly felt it's beating heart, even if at times it took some patience to listen to its gentle but steady murmur.

The streets were quiet at that early hour: a late spring morning, Union Street pierced through with the golden hues of a rising dawn. He feels lucky to witness it. Fortune favours the brave he was once told. He's unconvinced; maybe if you're patient enough luck will find its way to you. All he knows is on that day he was waiting for her and she appeared, on that morning, on that street, at that particular time.

He's seen a few characters cutting through the streets at this hour, many of them looking like they wouldn't know what luck is, let alone have had any share of it. The unfortunate few that sleep rough, just like in many other cities; he cannot imagine anything braver, and where is their fortune? He always takes the time to gently sweep and clean around them, often huddled under dirty blankets, faces hidden, burrowed deep into the shop entrances. Making sure not to wake them, he makes a point of giving any loose change he has. Dropping it into their old Starbucks cups or hats if they're still left out on the pavement. The numbers change according to the seasons, the warmer air making sleeping outdoors slightly less horrific, the city's famous flowers and foliage not the only earthly life to bloom in spring.

Then there are the workers, wearing their suits and ties, skirts and shirts, heels kept firmly under foot. Delivery vans unloading fruit, bread, and papers, everything fresh and new, yesterday's already discarded, already under his brush or in his bin, no use to anyone anymore.

Then there was her. Just another one of the early worker folk, a skirt and heels, a blazer and blue shirt, heading down Union Street to open a travel agent. Like she did every other day and yet somehow she had slipped past his eye, until this particular morning in the Granite City, shining and shimmering in its grey grandeur.

He couldn't imagine working for a travel agent, booking holidays for people, watching their excited faces as they confirm their sunny or exotic trip away. He was maybe a little envious, but folk worked hard for their cash and if they deserve a break away then good for them. He once went to Tenerife when he was a young man, with his mum, dad, aunties and uncles - it was a big thing, the first family holiday abroad. Auntie Marilyn already drunk and slurring as the wheels hit the tarmac, burnt rubber billowing into the air. Stepping off the plane into the late evening heat, the way it hit him like he'd been suddenly drugged, he'll never forget that. He'd love to go back, he's saved some wages, kept a bit aside each month over the past eight years, he was good like that, diligent. But single men in their forties don't go on holidays themselves, do they?

He watched as she walked along the opposite side of the street he was sweeping. In a rush and dropping her keys, flustered. As she picked them up she caught her reflection in a shop window. Checking her face and delicately placing a loose hair back behind her ear, she looked past her reflection and saw him watching. Embarrassed, she looked down quickly and placed the keys into her handbag. He almost couldn't get the words out of his mouth, his brain dead with awe.

"Dinnae worry, you look stunning."

A smile flashed across her face and immediately he could feel his chest expand and flutter. She walked on, probably not used to street sweepers having a tongue. Courage regained, he shouted.

"I'll get that windae cleaned so you can look again the morn if you need!"

At that, she stopped and laughed. Turning to him with a smile that could breathe life into any man condemned for eternity, she spoke.

"Bless you, you're too kind."

That was it. All it took. She was off again. The next day he booked a holiday to Tenerife.

Gavin Gilmour

Metamorphosis of Space

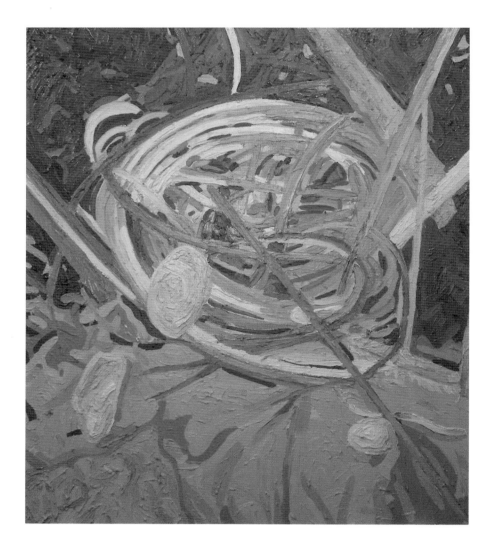

Katarina Chomova
oil-yacht-varnish-on-canvas
2D 1050 x 1200 mm

Saxicola torquata

What's in the gorse?
Shadow.

What's in the gorse?
Only shadow,
hidden.

What's in the gorse?
Only shadow,
hidden shadow,
skulking.

What's in the gorse?
No light.

What's on the gorse?
Listen.
Stones.

What's on the gorse?
Only stones,
river stones,
jostled.

What's on the gorse?
Only stones,
Jostled stones,
singing.

What's on the gorse?
Stone music.

Heather Reid

Aim

strange how it comes to this, the distant black astonished mouths
settling in a steady row, ready to spit oblivion.

                    Elizabeth standing by the upright piano,
                        cock-eyed red cross

the grass is trampled here, mud leaks through weedy fronds,
the dance-floor for a score of twitching men. St Vitas. Crispin Crispianus

                  the high pink smell of moor-top heather
            giant blades of granite
      curlew's siren hoot

in a split slice of a second, I glimpse a kestrel, black scratch in the
half-cooked sky, breathing a tower of air, dropping

            Elizabeth.
              black eye-lash on her white cheek

strange how I'll never touch

Who will tell her? A blank white hand with a telegram
afraid to say I shook like a marionette my bowels burned
they'll have to scrub the stench off the khaki later
when they cart what's left off my tongue pressing my palette my teeth
chattering my arms jerking as the clicks like children's
claps like nails on teeth dog's claws on pavements belt buckles
harness rings

                the kestrel drops
                  in a cloudless yellow dawn

                          through the scent of heather

Louise Wilford

Child

She sleeps,
fists pink and tight, flags furled.
A nameless dream is dribbling from her tongue.

Her hair's old bourbon brown, her breath is gold;
the veins that net her bones are lacework on the lids.

She tucks her fingers in between my lips,
a grappling hook against my teeth,
like I'm a tower she's climbing –
or her fingers are the barbed harpoon
gripping a whale she's caught.

The squash of her baby cheek against the sheet,
pinked in the night-light's earnest glow,
reminds me of far away and long ago.

She smells of sleep and sap,
of fairytales that trap her in the thorny
filigree of ancient forests,
pull tiny murmurs from her throat.

She's no blank page, this child I never had.
Her breath sighs out a thousand unheard words;
her mermaid eyes twitch with her unseen thoughts.

She wants to let me know she's here, and now.
It's in her head's slight twist,
in eyes that move inside their shell of skin,
in lips that mumble, wordless,

as she dreams my dreams.

Louise Wilford

Faces

One night, when our son was four years old, we heard him talking to himself in the middle of the night. His voice was an asyllabic drone which crept through the wall.

Curious, we rose from our bed and tip-toed to his room. Pressed our ears against the door. His words beat against the wood like summer rain. Pushing the door open with a gentle nudge, we found him hunched forward on his knees. In his little fists he held the teddy bear we had bought him for his birthday the week before. He continued mumbling but even at such close range we could not make out the words he was saying. If he had heard our approach he gave no sign of it but as the heat from our bodies warped the shape of the air he stopped, turned, and stared at us.

From his bed, we must have looked strange to him. Our bodies, cast in shadow by soft lamplight, contorted into misshapen monsters. Instead of asking why he was still awake, or why he was talking to his teddy bear, we whispered our love, and told him to go to sleep. We retreated. When the door clicked back into place we heard the mumbling begin again.

The next day, during breakfast, we said nothing. We waited for him to bring it up, casting wary eyes at each other above his head. The tension devoured us. I rubbed the sweat from my hands into the grooves of my chair.

We heard him mumbling again that night but this time we did nothing. Instead, we tried to sleep. It came easier to us than we expected. We resisted the urge to plant a recording device in his room. He would know, he would just know, we assured each other. In truth, we were terrified of what he might be saying.

A month passed before the mumbling stopped. We never found out why but we supposed he grew bored of it. He never fixed on any one thing for long. Our relief over the breakfast table confused him but again we said nothing.

One day, some time later, we went to tuck him into bed and found him singing songs out the open window. We asked who he sang to. Did he have a friend on the other side of the road? He laughed and said no, told us we were being silly. No, he said again, he wanted to be friends with the moon. Singing someone a song was the best way to become friends, he said. The moon was lonely and oh so far away. I grinned and ruffled his soft white hair. I do not know if the moon has many friends, I said, but he would be proud to have you as one.

When he began school, as all children must, the teacher told us he was doing well. He enjoyed maths and reading and hearing about the world. The teacher said he listened best when she was telling the class about space and the stars and the sky. He had some friends, she said, but not too many. That was okay. He was a good boy and no one made fun of him. She said on rainy days he liked to run off on his own into the wooded corners of the playground. There his friends would find him pushing his fingers through the mud, making faces in the earth's skin. Sometimes the faces were smiling, other times they were not. When the faces were sad he liked to tell them stories. Sometimes, he told the teacher, it was fun to cheer someone up.

At home he turned his attention from the moon to the stars. We frantically bought books and star charts and even a telescope. We sat by his window and told him their names. He liked to know their names. He learned how to find Orion's Belt and the Big Dipper. We showed him photographs of the Pillars of Creation and the Milky Way - our home. We read him the stories of the astrological signs. We learned as much as he did.

Growing bored of our stories, he began pointing at less familiar collections of stars. He raised a finger to the sky with an authority we could never command and said Look, Look! There's his legs and his body, there's his arms and his head. His name is Alex. Then he said Look, Look! There next to him are her legs and her body, her arms and her head. Her name is Jane. A dot-to-dot boy and a dot-to-dot girl made from the stars. He made up stories about them, about how they played together across the immeasurable expanse of infinity. We laughed and hugged him and called him a marvel. For weeks these stories came. He created a school of generous and happy boys and girls. The stories we told him didn't matter because his were always better.

He grew so fast. In the morning, as we scrambled over toast and untied shoes, we often caught him lingering in front of the mirror in his room. He would squint and move from side to side, then lean in and out. Sometimes he waved to himself, said hello to his reflection. When we helped him tie his shoes we caught him gazing off to the side, at the patterned carpet or the unevenly painted walls.

He ended up in a fight when he was seven. We were called in to the school. A boy had called him a weirdo, a loser. This, to our son, merited a punch. In return, he received two for his trouble. Soft round bruises bubbled under his cheek and around his eye. This was not like him, the teacher said, although it was part of a growing pattern of strange behaviour. She said he cried when it rained. Inconsolable tears of frustration and rage. He lingered in the classroom at break time, liked to play with the chalkboard and smack the dust around. When he did go outside he lay on the ground, even when it was cold, and stared at the clouds. He talked to himself a lot. We told her he wasn't talking to himself but to the clouds, the earth, the trees. Everything. He often did this instead of playing with his friends. Most of them had stopped talking to him. This didn't worry the teacher, boys and girls fell out all the time, what worried her was that he hadn't seemed to notice, or mind. He was happy but she didn't understand why. It is not too late to act, the teacher said, but she gave us no solid advice. It's not right, she said; it didn't seem wrong to us at all.

We found a box under his bed stuffed with pictures, paintings, photographs, print-outs from school, pages ripped from books. The images took on familiar forms: the Galle Crater on Mars; the Romanian Sphinx; the peaks of Pedra da Gavea; Franconia; the "Grimacing human face" in the Mercantour National Park; the Turin Shroud. There were doodles of cloud formations, ink blots, works by Giusseppe Arcimboldo. The deeper into the box we delved the less human the images became. Mere hints of facial structure, abstracted shapes with near-human identities. Mistakes the universe had made, close calls, near misses.

We asked him why he had these images, what they were for. He said they were faces. He found them interesting. There were faces everywhere. Not just on the bodies of people, or cats, or dogs, or elephants, but in plants, burned onto rocks, and in the sky. Everywhere.

Faces

Thousands and thousands of Janes and Alexes he could play with. By finding the faces he could make the world happier:

The more faces there were, the less the world scared him. The less sad he felt. It meant he was never alone. We asked, without imagination, if the faces spoke back. He said no. I asked if he wanted them to speak back. He said no. He wasn't expecting a reply. Not getting a reply was not a problem. That's not why people talked to each other.

His new teacher suggested we send him to a psychologist. His behaviour was disrupting his learning. It wasn't really a suggestion but we ignored her anyway. We thought he would change. He didn't. He developed.

Everything started to take twice as long to do. He talked to the faces in the carpet or the wall; we were used to this by now, but then he began to see faces in the folds of his clothes, in the grooves of his fingers. We could not see what he saw half the time. We didn't know who he was talking to anymore.

One morning when he was being uncooperative and I was running late for work I told him to stop it. I said, Son, there are no faces. Maybe they looked like faces but that was not the same thing. You cannot stop and talk to everything you see. You need to stop before you drive us insane. There are no faces. He burst into tears then he pushed me out the way, ran from me.

Worn out, we took him to see a doctor. For a while, things improved.

Puberty arrived and altered the shape of his body. He seemed to have forgiven me. By increments his behaviour changed. He spoke to the faces less and he spoke to us more. For a while there was nothing strange in his behaviour but soon we noticed that when he spoke, and we replied, his eyes would linger on the peripheries of our bodies: the shoulder blades, our necks, the empty spaces to the side of our faces. When we told him to do a chore or his homework he would pause for a second, as though the words had arrived in his head in the wrong order. He looked at the proximity of our faces, then gave an answer. The answers were always the ones we wanted to hear but we started to worry.

His speech began to change. Words became soft on his tongue, like damp bread, and he would spit them out into our upturned palms like a toddler. When we examined them they fell apart in our fingers. They crumbled in our ears no matter how delicately we pushed them in.

He started smashing the reflective surfaces in the house: televisions, mirrors, sinks. He took a marker pen to the ones he couldn't break. I hid the telescope in the attic before he unscrewed the lens cap. He told us his reflection scared him.

His teachers stopped asking him to answer questions in class. He tried, once, to explain to us that words were subjective. Words contained more information and less meaning than the objects they were assigned to describe. He said there was too much information. He was trying to be clear but he only had words to explain himself and words were not enough.

The psychologist chastised us. He said we lacked discipline. He told us to be stricter. We could not give in to the whims of our son. It was easier said than done. We didn't understand what he was doing until he did it and no one had an explanation for what was happening to him.

By the time he was fifteen his glazed eyes looked through us. When he entered a room we could not persuade him we were there. He walked with his hands held out in front of him like he had gone blind, his face emptied of expression. We stood next to him and held his fingers against our faces, spoke with comfort as his nerve endings measured the contractions and expansions of our lips as we spoke. It didn't help. I said It's me, Dad, but he remained unconvinced. He said the wind pressed shapes into the grooves of his fingers too. And how, really, was that different? He had drawn a line in the sand and we had let the wind smooth it over instead pulling him back across to our side.

He said he was scared of closing his eyes. Shadows waltzed across his eyelids, refusing to make identifiable shapes. They moved back and forth, closer and farther, without reason.

He became fussy and inexplicable around food. The motion of his fork made him seasick. He looked at the ceiling, at the corner of the room, as he ate.

His speech continued to thin, he communicated in windswept syllables, and we grew frantic. We asked him how we could help.

Weeks passed without a distinguishable word leaving his mouth. His speech dwindled into nothing. We began to create meaning from the way he breathed.

His teachers complained about his inhuman handwriting. They knew there was meaning in the lines he pressed into the paper but he could not explain himself. He could not be understood. We withdrew him from school.

He stood in the corner of his room, in silence, staring at the wall. The doctors told us to keep an eye on him at all times. He no longer responded to words or gestures. We held his arms and his back and led him into bed each night. We often heard him rising from his bed soon after. A shuffle of movement, back into the corner, then nothing. As language decayed inside him everything merged into one. We hoped that from this singularity the world would then unfold outwards before him like it did before a newborn baby but nothing changed. We kept vigil over his silence. The world shrank around us until it was the size of the house.

On the nights when he didn't rise from our gentle, guiding hands, we lingered in the door way like we had when he was little. We waited for his voice to fracture the silence but it never did. The silence grew, and from it a new language formed and with it we spoke the same four words to each other over and over again: What do we do? What do we do? What do we do? We had no answers. Words gave us no comfort. We finally understood what he meant when he told us that words were not enough.

Now, every night, when my wife wilts from a fatigue borne of exhaustion and helplessness she heads off to bed. I often join her, but on the nights when I can't sleep I climb the stairs to the attic where I have set up the telescope. There, with one eye pressed against the lens, I spend hours tracing back and forth across the sky hoping to find Alex and Jane, or Peter and Kara, or Harry and Roseanne, any of the dot-to-dot friends he had created as a child. Hoping that if I find them I can find the world our son had made. A world which we had lived in for so long. I believed for so long that if I could find his world I could find him, and within his world I could explain to him, in a language he understood, the errors I have made and the grief I feel over words I wish I could take back. With these words I would bring him back to us. But through the endless repetition of my search I have realised that his world is lost to him, just as he, our world, is lost to us. Then, when exhaustion takes hold, or I grow frustrated with endlessly recalibrating the stars, or the sun begins to rise over the rooftops, I drag myself down from the attic, push open the door to my son's room with a gentle nudge, tiptoe across the floor, and kneel down at his bedside. There, in the only language I have, I whisper to him the only words I have left: I love you. I am sorry. I was wrong.

Ross McCleary

Contour

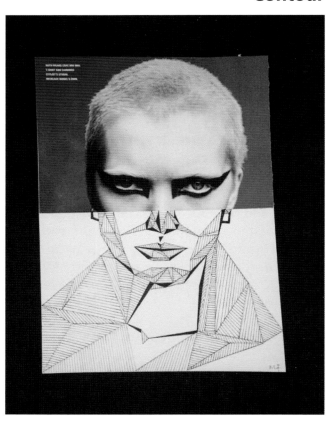

Xiaoyu Fan
Colour / collage
2D 210 x 297 mm

Planting Level

When they came to visit, Dad worked
his middle-aged sons hard,
all day. Ninety-one years
allowed him this privilege,
a yard the size of a small town
earned him this right.

The boys tilled miles of uneven grass,
dug post holes, strung wire,
flung shit into rows for planting.
Dad went to every nursery in town
for herbs, flowers, tomatoes.

Every jarred spice in the wobbly
kitchen drawer was from decades past.
Can't make pasta without basil,
so grow it fresh. No marinara
without tomatoes...

and honor your wife with Rose of Sharon
and poppies.

The sons - flecked with dirt
and bloodied calluses,
worn out for the first time
since high school football,
were collapsed in the showers,

water running sweaty,
reviving nothing.

Tools back in their appointed spots,
Dad watched the twilight ravel down
the day in his new garden, camp chair
solid on straight earth, hoarse from shouting orders,
the warm relief of Drambuie on ice.

He took stock of the new plants, the fence line,
the boundary. A nod for a job well done,
for what takes so long to measure.

Tobi Alfier

My Family Tree

At the bottom of our garden stands a grand and ancient tree,
which was planted by our ancestors in 1683
and ever since that day it has improved our circumstances
for we haven't got a house, you see, we live upon the branches.

Great Grandpa Jack and Great Gran Mary sleep among the roots.
They don't move much, but still they're game for all sorts of pursuits.
Mary is a pudding chef, she's well known for her trifle,
Jack sends local squirrels nuts then shoots them with his rifle.

Around the corner of the stump, or so we think at least,
Great Uncle Jeremiah lives: a great and shaggy beast.
His hair and fingernails are thirteen times the length of mine
and he hasn't cleaned beneath his beard since 1989.

On the lower branches, Grandpa Pete smokes cigarettes
much to the ire of Nana Jo who fusses, fumes and frets.
I wish you'd give it up, she says, *you'll die of some disease!*
At least, my dear, he says with cheer, *we don't get stung by bees.*

Across from them is Grandma Em still dressed in widow's weeds –
the bough below her buckles from the pile of books she reads.
She's captive reading classics, she won't leave her rocking chair,
and over time the sparrowhawks have nested in her hair.

Mum and Dad have filled their branch with more than I can mention:
a games room, salon, study and they've plans for an extension!
They're calling in a joiner, plumber and an architect
for a fancy annexe finished with a genuine wood effect.

One branch up my siblings, grotty Gill and rotten Russell,
try to knock the other landwards in a daily treetop tussle.
The family far below them know that every night they will
have to catch airborne descendants – sometimes Russell, sometimes Gill.

And me, I'm on the very top – the star on Christmas Day!
The little one, the most important - oh, and by the way,
if you think I'm like my family then I'd have to disagree,
but they say an apple never settles too far from the tree.

Richie Brown

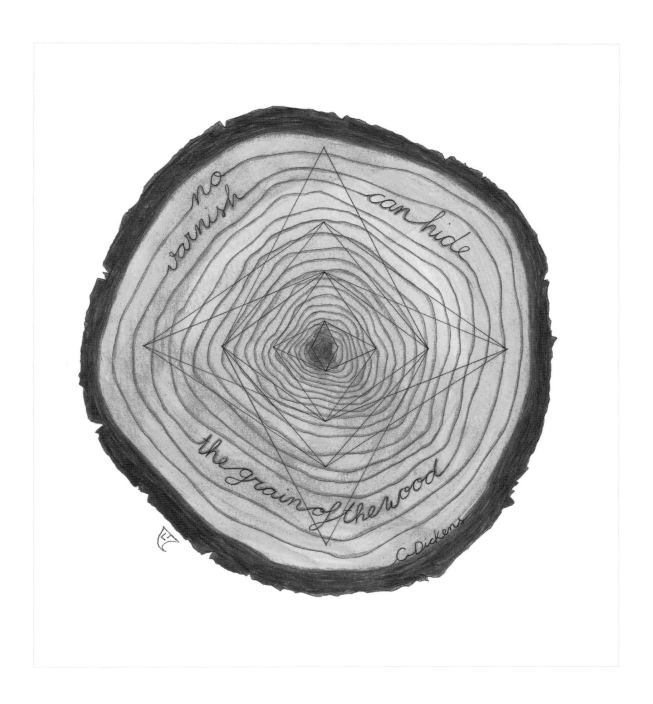

Lady Thornfield
Colour / Acrylic
2D 210 x 285 mm

Midnight on the Estuary

A shadow slips unnoticed along the dockway. Moored fast to a solid iron cleat, a small wooden boat bobs in the water as the figure places a number of large chests in the hull. Looking out over the waters, he shivers. *The currents are strong lad, unforgiving; I've seen them sweep many a good man out to sea...* Once his father's, the words now echo around emptily in his head: *currents strong...many a good man...swept out to sea...*

Clutching the beacon in his hand, he looks behind him, surveying the docks, its landscape of giant, inhuman structures. He sees the silhouettes of monstrous cranes that by day pick truck-sized containers and stack them neatly like blocks of Lego; he looks at the ships waiting to be loaded, the vast open spaces of decks the size of football pitches, then up at the crew's quarters, towering above like a block of flats. He imagines the men alone on the seas, the lights on the ship's mast flashing in the dead of night, sending out signals into the oblivion, like remote transmissions from a distant planet, swallowed up in the emptiness of an infinite space. A skeleton crew, pushing on through icy waters, abandoned to the intensity of their collective solitude; miles from nowhere, miles from home.

He remembers the wistful gaze in his father's eyes. He would see it sometimes when he was back in port, occasionally catching him off-guard as he stared vacantly into the fire. He looks along past the ships and his eyes are caught by a sudden movement. He strains at the darkness, scanning the forecastles. Shadows, he thinks, just shadows; there can't possibly be anyone here at this time of night. Yet he knows he needs to remain wary nonetheless. Clipping the beacon to his jeans, he starts climbing the ladder, gripping the cold steel of the handrail, his heavy boots catching firmly on the rungs. Within a few minutes it will be lit and a tiny green light will beam out over the estuary from atop the mast, piercing the night sky; then he will descend and make his way over to the boat to await the signal from the other side.

Freeing the rope from its cleat, he pushes off, backing the stern carefully out of the slip. The silence is broken by the gentle splash of his oars as they lick the surface of the water. He manoeuvres the vessel so the bow is pointing out towards the estuary. Taking a deep breath, he surveys the line of buoys tracing a path out into the open water. *...many a good man...* Faded fluorescent pinks and oranges that seem to glow brighter than normal in the night. *...swept out to sea...* His eyes dart back to the lights of the docks. Slowly, he enters out onto the silky, quicksilver surface, lit only by the steely glare of the moon. He starts to feel the current's pull. He rows and, as he does so, he remembers his father's face, weather-beaten and charred from years of exposure to the ravages of the wind. He remembers his wispy grey beard, the weary look in his eyes. He sees them staring dully into the fire, the old man's power of sight long since gone. He watches the wizened hands as they grapple with his papers, struggling to make himself a smoke. *...our past is out there son, it's out there in the sea...* He remembers his father's tales. He sees the ships on the horizon, longboats of sturdy Norse pine, manned by rude Scandinavian warriors who will come to savage the lands and leave behind them an indelible mark on the people and their words. But those boats sail on into the night and are succeeded instead by the criss-crossing paths of medieval vessels, journeying between coarse ports, bringing wool to Flanders and the sea's fruits to France, returning home laden with delicacies from abroad. Their paths linger in luminescent traces, suspended momentarily above the surface of the water, the vessels' shapes shifting like holograms in the moonlight, rising up from the sea then sinking back into its depths. He can hear the voice of a thrice-betrayed pirate setting sail to guard the spoils of empire, unaware that upon his return he will receive not a hero's welcome but that of a traitor, hanged and gibbeted for all to see. Then come the ships turning home from a far-off land, the heads of the crews bowed low, shamed at their failure to follow where others have gone before them, eventually passing out of sight, consigning their dreams of prosperity and grandeur to the past, leaving a lugubrious silence in their wake.

Raeburn rows, haunted by confused images from his father's tales, haunted by visions of a past of which he is unable to make sense. If only I could, he thinks, if only I could make sense... But instead he is distracted by the words of a childhood song, a sweet, mellifluous voice that fills the air: 'Speed bonnie boat like a bird on a wing...' Two fine ladies, laden with hopes and dreams, unaware of the cruel fate one day to be suffered at the butcher's hands. 'Carry the lad that was born to be king...' But history had other plans, and early one morning the lad would instead slip stealthily from the isles, out onto the sea to die in exile, a bonnie wee prince who would never be king. Raeburn looks around him. The water is still; he can feel the gentle tug of the current. He rows defiantly against it. He can see the lighthouses flashing in the darkness, their mute conversation, indecipherable pulses of a demonic Morse code that spans the globe. He imagines the earth out there in space, spinning on its axis; he imagines it without the sun, spinning alone in an eternal darkness. Black is the night and black are the seas, their surface swiftly ruffled by a sinister gust of wind which blows, snuffing out the lights of the lighthouses one by one, reducing that infernal chatter to silence, until all that remains is a single, solitary beacon, flashing boldly in the darkness, stark atop the forgotten crags of a rocky islet at the world's end, the icy waters of the Antarctic swirling down below. Then he can hear his father's voice once again: *the sea has blood son - when you prick it, it bleeds; just see what they're doing son, just look how we've let them bleed us dry...*

The ghostly shapes of suited vampires rise up from the water until they loom large in the night, towering over Raeburn and his small rowboat, peering down upon him with zombie eyes in whose sockets he sees not eyeballs but pound signs, lambent, jaundiced, yellowy light. They chomp cigars, their fangs drip slimy black blood that oozes down their suits and spreads out in a toxic slick over the surface of the water, suffocating the life below. And meanwhile, on the other side of the land, giant metal ships set forth to sail the seas: one by one, they are sent down the slipways, plunging into the water, their metal bodies kicking up a mighty swaw, bound tightly by rivets that for some are just pieces of metal, but which for others are much much more: stitching together whole communities of workers and their kin, binding together the hopes and dreams of thousands of the undeniable right to a more just world, one in which there will be nae bevvyin, just blood, sweat and toil; just graft and struggle, a futile, uphill struggle; the story of those who find themselves forever against the grain.

The current quickens. As he rows Raeburn ponders the fate of those men, until distracted by a line of buoys, then a second, the two tracing convergent paths through the water, their garish, psychedelic colours burning in the night, searing the retinas of his eyes, drawing his gaze on into the distance, on to where there stands a giant metal bridge, resplendent in the darkness, effulgent with thousands of tiny golden lights. The sound of a foghorn booms out across the water and a tremendous juggernaut appears: fearless, twelve thousand, one hundred and twenty tonnes of metal, her propellers churning at the seas, drawing him along in their wake. Full speed ahead! He can hear the cackle of the captain, she too made of iron, standing proudly at the helm. He tries to scream above the roar, but no sound emerges from his mouth, or if it does it is swallowed whole by the din of the ship's engines. The waters froth and swirl. The ship thunders on, continuing on what he suddenly realises to be a collision course with one of the bridge's stone supports. He knows then it will fall. He looks up in horror to meet the eyes of the moribund workers gazing out from the top, out over waters littered with fragments of the past, a kaleidoscope of confused and fragmented images. If only, he thinks, we could make sense... If only we could organise somehow... the images, ourselves. He prays for the ship to turn, but knows she's not for turning. Powerless, impotent, dragged along in the wake, he consigns himself to the impending catastrophe. If only, he thinks, if only we could...

Then suddenly the air gives an almighty shudder, erupting with the din of crunching stone, the groans of buckling girders, the low-pitched wails from the falling bodies. And the sea swallows the scene whole, its waters thrashing furiously, consuming the illusions as the warship limps on into the night, its captain cackling, her figure silhouetted against a full moon. Then the water grows calm once more; the storm abates. The rowboat comes to a halt with a gentle bump, embedding itself in the sand, small waves trickling on past it, on towards the shore, their delicate crests gushing peacefully, continuing for a couple of metres past the boat before washing up on the land.

James Kelly

Storm

Kiki Callaghan *[Aged 15]*
Acrylic
2D 394 x 368 mm
Winner of our Young Artist Award

My Sister is Dying

Do you feel the cold Bernie? I ask
as she comes in from the garden's warmth with a thick cardigan on.
She turns her strange eyes in my direction.
And for a moment, I think I see something move there, behind them.

Well, what the fuck do you think?   she might have said.
Or
Do you dare to ask me that here?   That I might tell you the answer.

But that moment passes silently.
It is like the child who was taken out the back
and held under the water
while the rest of the family ate at table.
Nor did he struggle, only a few reflexive spasms.
And I respond in kind to her sensible answer.

Like a Fist

My father was a tall man
And I the child in his shadow.
There was something dark about him
Like a loaded fist.
Or teeth scattering suddenly on lino
With a mouth that tastes of blood.

One day in late December,
Without any warning,
My mother's voice,
Coming from the telephone in the public call box,
Said *Your Dad is dead.*
As I walked back past the bakers,
Suddenly,
My stomach had no bottom.
But I caught it
With the fists my father gave me.

Jim Conwell

Muse & Rapture

I didn't notice Mieke at first. There were dozens of music students passing through the exhibition space, arriving in laughing gaggles to try the early instruments and declare themselves astonished at how good they were, considering... She stood alone, three yellow volumes of Bach's *Harpsichord Works* tucked under one arm. She was quite still near the back of the room, oblivious to people moving around her as they paused to listen. There were three other viol players beside me settling to play. I didn't know them but the way they handled the instruments, tuning swiftly and across chords, showed they were experienced players. I had some four-part Lassus on the stands, simple enough to sight-read but requiring a grasp of their idiomatic form – otherwise they were just lines of crotchets.

We began with my nod. I happened to look up at our closing chord and the following rapt silence and saw her swaying slightly, apparently sleeping on her feet. Afraid she might faint (she looked about 13-years-old and I remembered my own adolescent absences) I was about to alert R, my husband, to go to her, when she opened her eyes. They were full of tears. My companions were speaking to me, admiring the music, noting its publisher, proud to have made such a sound, but I hardly heard them. She was moving forward now against the flow of the audience and by the time she had reached me, the room was almost empty again. She had brushed away the tears and her eyes were bright with excitement.

"May I?" she asked, so quietly I didn't realise what she was asking for, so she indicated the bass viol lying on its side and repeated, "May I?"

I sat her down astride the instrument. She apologised for the shortness of her skirt and said she would wear something more suitable tomorrow. She handed the Bach to R and I handed her a bow and showed her with mine how to coax the warm plangent tone from the gut string. She scraped. I left her to it for a while. You have to find your own way into the viol.

If he had been born into ancient Greece, R would have naturally had a lyre in his hands while he sang, or on his back while he walked to his next performance. As it was he was born in the post war 1940s and came of musical age through the BBC Third Programme, school singing and his father's mostly good piano and organ playing. Then one day he heard The Shadows and while his heart found a hero in Hank Marvin, his body and soul were possessed by the sound of the electric guitar. He was undersized, acutely self-conscious, alternately championed and over-protected by his formidable mother and intimidated by his father, who made it clear to R that he was, in some indefinable sense, a disappointment. This was not music but a hell of a racket. A fab racket, thought R, but didn't say so. He was spellbound but no matter how many hours he spent in front of the mirror playing air guitar before anyone called it that, he knew he was not quite the stuff of rock stars. But he was a maker.

No-one knew where R's empathy with wood came from. His father knew how things worked and what they should look like but not how to be inside making them which was how R spent his days, measuring and cutting, planing and smoothing pieces of wood. His mother thought, lovingly and indiscriminately, everything he did was touched with God's grace. These were the gentle years of post-war education, liberal enough to nurture the slow and careful alongside the quick and the clever. R was slow but his depth of understanding of how things go together and stay together flowed in him like his blood and was just as vital to his life. Tables and toast-racks he made as a child still function in our house. So, when R fell in love with the electric guitar and his father wouldn't buy him one, he did what came naturally and made his own.

Mieke stayed for an hour the first time. I showed her the notes of Tallis' *Canon*. Stiffened with will power, she put her head down and forced them into her hands, onto the bow and off the strings. It was very simple but it sounded awful. She shook her cramped left hand in the air. She was near tears again.

"Why does it sound so bad?" she asked. "It sounded like heaven when you played."

"You're trying to play the whole sequence. Try just one string, two notes, move from one to the other."

I felt awkward. I am a self-taught player, have little or wayward technique and no training. All I have is my love of R's viols and renaissance music. Mieke was at the exhibition demonstrating another maker's harpsichords, playing Bach on a raised platform in the main hall in front of hundreds of people. In that slight body and nimble fingers resided knowledge and patterns of musical movement far in excess of what she was trying to do. She was, however, well versed in the role of pupil. She fell to bowing a single string over two, then three notes, over and over and then she was smiling, finding the gentleness in her arms and hands that worked *with* the viol. She played the opening four notes of the canon and grinned at me. I played the next four at the same time. We had a harmony. Suddenly she looked at her watch.

"Oh no, my next demonstration," she gasped. "Can I come back?"

Eagerly, so eagerly, she grabbed her books of Bach and disappeared.

Passion makes up for a lot. Like other early-sixties teenagers they were not rich, free and uninhibited though they talked about such states with great conviction. R's school band met in the cellar, courtesy of the divorced mother of one of them, and played on rough instruments with bodged together fittings and intermittent amplifiers that smelt of hot electric wiring. Their repertoire was everything with guitars in it. There was some jostling for position between hopeful members. R saw the writing on the wall and became a bass guitarist because he liked working with the drummer, and the other lead guitarist was more showy than he was. Besides, they had invitations to play at village hops and he wasn't going to be left out. School days were coming to a close and R's raucous nighttime band members were heading towards daytime university or jobs. As soon as they left, the head of the music department promptly forbade the formation of rock bands but they hung onto the band as long as they could.

Later there were changes in the line-up as the band evolved and started to play the university circuit. R started to meet other players who excited him, started to go to concerts in London, saw Ginger Baker and Jack Bruce, worshipped Hendrix. The possibilities for betrayal of old friends were many as R chased the purity of the music. He couldn't be unfaithful to the velvet throb of his Fender though he ditched his school band drummer with only mild regret. He spent hours listening intently to the radio, isolating the bass lines, memorising them and playing them. This was more difficult at concerts. There was a lot of dope about. Too much, too many lost nights. R, clutching his woodwork teacher's certificate, fled north to a school like the one he had flourished in, and took up folk music.

On the hour she was back. The room was full with prospective musicians, some of them customers. She slipped quietly through to the music boxes and examined the pieces carefully. No single piece in our collection would demand the theoretical grasp or agility of the simplest pieces in her *Bach Studies*, but she was absorbed in her reading. Now and then she held a book up and whispered to me.

"Is this one nice?"

Groups formed, played and disbanded around her. A lunchtime lull drained them away and she hopped into the chair and took up the viol again. This time we made it through the opening three phrases of Tallis' *Canon*, together, then one after the other. R joined us, adding a third voice and saying to her, "You just keep playing those three phrases."

She bent her head, the most diligent of students, whilst we played the whole canon before, with and behind her. Another musician, still in his outdoor coat, quietly took the fourth seat and dropped into the tune behind Mieke, departing some strains later in the middle of playing, leaning across and saying "Thank you, my dears", but especially to her. She, bravely, inserted the fourth sequence and succeeded, her frown locked to the struggle in her fingers. She laughed out loud.

We stopped for lunch, just sandwiches, we couldn't leave the instruments. She told us about herself. She was nineteen, going to America on a music scholarship, home tutored, her brother too – shy, but who played beautiful cello – but these viols, these beautiful viols, why had she never seen one before? Then she had to go again.

"Can I come back?" her plaintive sigh.

R was more practical than I. "As long as there's no-one new waiting to try the instruments." He sounded harsh, but he was there to sell instruments.

"Very well. Of course," she said and slipped away. She didn't come back that day.

R worked at making viols with an eclectic soundtrack, sometimes silky folk guitar, sometimes dirty blues and latterly the hugely amplified sound of jazz-funk with its humming, orgasmic bass lines. He played this very loud into the peaceful landscape outside his workshop. He didn't know about Clapton but he thought that Jaco Pastorius was as near to God as dammit.

Then, one off-duty weekend, late rising and the radio playing, he heard something that resonated inside him just as his Hank Marvin epiphany had. He stood still in the centre of his room listening to something he had never heard before, the sound of shawms and sackbuts and drums playing a dance tune. Like, but not like folk music; like, but not like classical music; like, but not like rock music. It was David Munrow rediscovering renaissance music. Within months R had a set of recorders, a year later crumhorns and cornamusen which he played with all and any musicians and instruments that were willing to join him in a splendid motley of styles and idioms, chasing that sound. Discovering that it was part music he had heard on the radio, he also discovered, with a blues player's natural disdain, that he needed to learn to read music. He also needed a 'proper' bass instrument. He decided to make a viol.

Years of guitar making, and his training as a furniture maker, meant his making activities had been uninterrupted from age four to thirty. What was a viol but a sort of bowed guitar? How hard could it be? He wrote to anyone and everyone he had heard of who had ever made a viol and collected a vast file of contradictory advice. He bought a kit and adapted it, applying what he knew made a good guitar to what he guessed would make a good viol. By the end of one long blissful summer holiday in his school workshop, he had his first instrument. He didn't know what the bow should be like or how he should hold it, so he extemporised.

Next day, the last day of the exhibition, Mieke came ten minutes after opening. She was wearing a long full skirt and carried a different set of keyboard studies. She explained she would have to leave at lunchtime, going back to Edinburgh on the Sunday train; so, could she play a little more? A Dutch musician, fairly well known, had promised to drop by later to play some virtuoso Ortiz. She would need a chordal accompaniment. R asked Mieke if she knew the blues. She laughed, taking him for tease but he took up his renaissance guitar and played a twelve bar blues on it.

"But not for the viols?" she asked.

"Yes, for the viols, but not these chords."

He opened the Ortiz score and showed her the chords of the *passamezzo moderno* laid out in four parts. She was astride her viol in a moment working out the sequence of one of the parts. R and I played alongside her, I doubled her part until she was confident, then I played another part.

Monique arrived. Flamboyant and funny, carrot-haired Monique came each year to wrap herself around R's viols and coax them into a very un-English excess of expression. R was a little in love with Monique's once a year uninhibited presence. Mieke gazed at her wide-eyed.

"Hello, honey." Monique threw the greeting into the air while she assembled her playing kit - viol, bow, rosin and music - and announced "*Ricercarda Secunda*." R took up his guitar and we began to play.

And there it was. Something of all of us thrown together to make something greater than its parts. R's rhythmic pulses drawn from every music that had ever thrilled him, Monique's extrovert and elaborate air carving of the melody, my simple love of harmony and Mieke... Mieke seemed to discover something ecstatic not experienced by solo players: the companionship of ensemble. She and I played our simple chord sequences over and over while the melody danced on around us. The sound drew people into the room to stand, not still but nodding and swaying gently, as if it were a rock concert and they had just identified the beat. At the finish, Monique swept to her feet, as was her right, to bow to their enthusiastic clapping; but, for anyone watching closely, it was clear that it was Mieke's triumph. She sat as if melted into her seat and she was humming softly, the large viol held in her calves like a lover.

"I must go," she said. "My train..."

We gave her a brochure. She promised to email us from America. The afternoon was choked with other players. They came alone to play the viols with strangers or with friends with whom they were comfortable. My fingertips ached with constant playing. Though I chose music and allocated instruments, my mind was elsewhere, dwelling on the slight figure of a girl who studied and revered the glories of Bach. We knew that other feeling , R and I, that moment when a renegade sound invades the bloodstream and starts up an endless dance. We knew what tune Mieke was humming as she went home to Edinburgh.

Vivien Jones

Hanging Around

Helen Forrest
Mixed Media on Board
2D 20 x 20 mm

Astraea X

Neil Russell
Colour / Collage
2D 210 x 295 mm

Differential Equations

Each time I have you figured out
sure as Rene Descartes' rule of signs,
confident I've cracked the algebraic code.
The sequence breaks up and falls apart.
You laugh at my laws of probability
and ridicule my reliance on statistics.
As you turn around, hair cascading into chaos,
parabolic curves swing in pendulum time,
your delicate hands rip at my pages of numbers
flinging them airborne, the butterfly effect.
All of my vectors and complex analysis,
all of my carefully worked proofs, redundant.
As you whisper quietly in my ear,
You're as easy as one and one makes two.

James Sinclair

Near Todleth

in a field of docks rain falls on us

        here are white hanks of sheepswool
            pegged like washing
                between drying posts

we breathe in lanolin and damp

        by clouded reeds a tatty ewe
            lurches away with her twins
                her off-fore lame

her bag all lumpy with mastitis

        you said it wouldn't last
          we follow
              an orange tip butterfly over the stile

Jean Atkin

Four Ways of Looking at a Crossroads

The cart slowly rumbles through ruts
Towards the crossroads.
A figure hangs, crow-pecked and tattered.
Daddy, why is that man...?
The driver reads milestones...
He stole bread.

...and drives right through wraiths
Of ceilidh seekers
All wondering where the craich is tonight.
As many as the spokes of a wheel are the choices
A man can make, he muses.

In time of war they take away the signs.
It is good to pause at a crossroads:
Feel for the safety of the lights,
The flavours of terrain,
See the trodden, watch the birds' flight,
Mark your cautious hesitation... to be sure...

For there is no map of paths
And all these destinations are the same.
More than twice the count of stars in the sky
Have I split – sent my body this way and that;
I dangle, gently swinging from a wire;
Dance and drink *usquebaugh* in a neighbour's croft.
The cart turns left and it turns right.

Clive Donovan

Hello I

collage and acrylic on paper
2D 170 x 125 mm

Calgary

digital photograph
2D 2848 x 2136 mm

Both Images by **Karen Beattie**

Different

Max opens the book he calls memory,
peels tattered covers back,
tries to wake sleeping words on the pages.
His mind is fingers brushing
across a long tongue of time.
He flips over to age twelve
where he is swaddled
in a worn green comforter
stripping paint from the ceiling with his eyes.
Outside, other boys play football.

Curious how this day is bookmarked
in his mind: the fever, the way he falls
asleep with a river in his hand.
Dry waves cover the streams of his lifelines.
Somewhere across the clouds
an arthritic musician licks the reed
of his honeyed clarinet.

Loretta Walker

Ward (Again)

Between the comfy chair
and the poison bated

the oven-hot room
and the needle's silver

the un-ignoring
just blood in your arm

the smile of the nurse
your own managed smile

the three-hour chat
with the neighbouring baldy

idly eyeing
a wig for its seam

is the paradox of
live minutes of dying

fights against death –
we're all skulls here.

Thomas Rist

What He Does and Doesn't Say

... must be the same family,
though they don't show in the 1830 census.

She nods her head, but she's not listening.
She studies strawberries in the bowl,
so ripe, so sweet this early in the season;
holds one under cold water, rubs at seeds,
lifts cap with her thumbnail,
simpler and quicker than the knife.

He's still talking.

She slices berries into a bowl,
sprinkles sugar to draw juices:
how good they'll be over ice cream.

He's still talking:
Walthan, you know, is an unusual name.

And she's still not listening, frowns
at a thumbnail so deep red it's almost black.
She dips a swab in lemon juice to clean it.

Still, he's talking.

Why, she wonders, does he talk
about people we don't know, we'll never meet,
and say not a single word
about anything affecting us?

Ann Howells

Spinal

Eilidh Morris
Chalks
2D 317 x 431 mm

Anchored

Southbound towards Aberdeen

granite rises beyond sailing dunes

and the North Sea spills

under whale back clouds.

Then a ritual: today we count

twenty-three oil workers

chain down in the bay

a pilot's call from harbour.

Berthed, their spires merge

tied together by the need

to belong somewhere

when water swallows the sun.

Bernard Briggs

Blue House, Hong Kong.

Jane Pettigrew
Watercolour
2D 210 x 300 mm

Contributor Information

Tobi Alfier is a multiple Pushcart nominee. *Down Anstruther Way*, a collection of Scotland poems, is just out from FutureCycle Press. She is co-editor of *San Pedro River Review* (www.bluehorsepress.com).

Jean Atkin has published *Not Lost Since Last Time* (Oversteps Books) also pamphlets and a novel. Her recent work appears in *Magma, Envoi, The North, Earthlines* and *The Moth*. www.jeanatkin.com

Rosie Bassett lives and works in Perth. She is a professional member of Visual Arts Scotland & writes poetry with the Soutar Writers. Combining words with illustration is her focus. www.visualartsscotland.org

Karen Beattie, a visual artist practising in North-East Scotland, graduated with a BFA in painting from Alberta College of Art & Design in Western Canada in 2013.

Sheena Blackhall is a writer, illustrator, traditional ballad singer and storyteller in North-East Scotland. In 2009 she became Makar (poet laureate) for Aberdeen and the North East.

John Bolland writes novels, poetry and short fiction. His work has appeared in a number of magazines and anthologies. He is a member of the Aberdeen Writers' Studio.

Nathan Breakenridge is 23 and lives in Alloa. He recently completed an MLitt in creative writing at the University of Stirling. He's not quite sure what to do next. *[This is Nathan's first published work- Ed]*

Bernard Briggs has been writing poetry for over 40 years. Since moving to Scotland in 2003 he has produced three collections & been published in various magazines & anthologies.

Richie Brown writes poetry and short stories from a secret location in Darkest Aberdeenshire. His pamphlet *Travel with my Rants* (Blue Salt, 2014) contains 21 puns.

Douglas Bruton won The Neil Gunn Memorial prize in 2015, the William Soutar Prize in 2014 and HISSAC in 2008. Recently he has been published by *Aesthetica, Northwords Now [& POTB – Ed]*.

Kiki Callaghan is a young artist residing in Aberdeen. In 2016 she was shortlisted in the National Open Art Competition and also included in an exhibition at Jack Tierney Gallery *[& Kiki wins our Young Artist Award - Ed]*

Nicola Chambury lives in Crathes and since the flood along the River Dee on 30 December 2015 has been working on etchings and monoprints arising from this experience.

Katarina Chomova, an Aberdeen artist, encompasses the idea of abandonment in her work. By carefully layering string she changes the spaces, deconstructing & reconstructing, using forms & shapes that inspire her.

Jim Conwell has worked in mental health for thirty years. He has published extensively in magazines and had two poems shortlisted for the Bridport Poetry Prize 2015. He lives in London.

Claire Cooper specialises in darkroom photography. She graduated from Grays School of Art in 2015 and is now studying towards her Masters in Medical Art at the University of Dundee.

Seth Crook loves puffins and has taught philosophy at various universities. His poems appear in *New Writing Scotland, Gutter, Northwords Now, Poetry Scotland, Causeway, Southlight, Raum, The Rialto* and elsewhere.

Clive Donovan devotes himself full time to poetry and has had poems published in magazines including *Agenda, Acumen, Interpreters House* and *Salzburg Review*. He has yet to make a first collection.

David Elder is a writer and photographer. His work includes *Cheltenham in Antarctica* (www.reardon.co.uk), and *Glenesk: the collected poems of John Angus*. www.invermarkbooks.co.uk

Mila [Xiaoyu] Fan, born in Urumqi city, China, currently resides in Scotland. Her artworks are inspired by the combination of business studies and daily life. Her first group exhibition was in 2016.

Helen Forrest paints from the heart. Vibrant colour, simple form and a creative use of texture are woven together to give her paintings their unique quirky quality. www.helenforrestgallery.co.uk

Pascale Free is a French, English and Spanish teacher. She loves writing and has been short- and long-listed for the Bridport and Fish short story competitions. This is her first publication.

Yani Georgieva is a radio journalist, a poetry writer, and a dog-petting enthusiast. She likes waffles and news and takes routine trips between Varna, Beirut and Aberdeen, looking for home.

Eddie Gibbons had a poem in Issue 1 of *Pushing Out the Boat*. Lots of wonderful and exciting things have happened since then, though not to him.

Gavin Gilmour is a Scottish writer based in Aberdeen, with a background in filmmaking and media production. He writes screenplays, plays and prose fiction *[and this is his first accepted publication – Ed]*

Lily Gontard lives in Yukon, Canada. Her writing has appeared in many publications. Her non-fiction book *Beyond Mile Zero*, about the Alaska Highway lodge community, will be launched in 2017.

Mandy Haggith is an award-winning poet, novelist and editor. Her most recent poetry collection is *A-B-Tree*. www.mandyhaggith.net

Robert Lee Haycock grew up in California's Santa Clara Valley - The Valley of Heart's Delight, and now resides in Antioch, California - The Gateway to the Delta.

Contributor Information

Ann Howells had a great 2016 that included three releases: *Under a Lone Star* (Village Books); *Letters for My Daughter* (Flutter); and as editor: *Cattlemen & Cadillacs* (Dallas Poets Community).

Vivien Jones writes poetry, short stories and drama. She has four collections in print. In 2016 she led several writing projects and is currently compiling a third poetry collection.

James Kelly is a translator by trade & has spent the last ten years going back and fore between Scotland & Chile. You can read more of his work at blog.geosoph.scot

Ross McCleary is from Edinburgh. He has a book published by Maudlin House Press. He also helps run Inky Fingers and edits podcast journal *Lies, Dreaming*.

Ian McDonough was raised in Brora, Sutherland, and lives in Edinburgh. His fourth collection - *A Witch Among The Gooseberries* - was published in November 2014 by Mariscat.

Susan Miller, a member of Huntly and Mearns Writers' groups, writes in English and Doric. A keen observer, her teaching, family and the outdoors all stoke her 'screivins'.

Ken Morlich is an Edinburgh-based writer whose work has been published in several anthologies and the odd magazine. He likes tank top cardigans. http://kmorlich.weebly.com/

Eilidh Morris is a Dundee-based visual artist who enjoys creating surreal artwork from her imagination, as well as nature art and portraits. She also has an interest in writing fiction.

Maxine Rose Munro is a Shetlander adrift on the outskirts of Glasgow, Her work has appeared in *Sarasvati, Open Mouse* and *Obsessed with Pipework,* among others. Find her here http:\\facebook.com/maxinerosemunro

Lynda Nash lives in Wales where she works as a creative practitioner. She is the author of *Ashes Of A Valleys Childhood* and *Not As Pointless As You Think*.

Jane Pettigrew, born Aberdeen, post-graduate of Gray's School of Art, has had a lifelong fascination with the urban environment. See more at www.masterpieceartstudio.com

Mark Regester was born in Scotland and raised in California, where he got his start making photographs of the local punk rock/skateboarding scene in the late 80's. He currently lives in St. Louis, Missouri.

Heather F Reid lives in Perthshire where she is a member of Soutar Writers. Her writing is best described as sporadic although she has had work published and broadcast on BBC radio.

Thomas Rist lectures on literature at the University of Aberdeen. A cancer gave rise to several poems including *Ward (Again)*. Thomas is now well. He continues to write.

Neil Russell lives and works in rural Aberdeenshire. An interest in fragmented and collaged text has led inevitably to the use of imagery, opening up seemingly endless possibilities...

Helena Sanderson draws inspiration mainly from history and the natural world. She is a poet, scriptwriter and student. She grew up on a Scottish island and currently resides in Cumbria.

Hamish Scott is from Edinburgh and writes poetry and prose in Scots. He has published three collections of his poetry with The Laverock's Nest Press.

Peter Sheal lives in Aberdeenshire and worked in the international oil industry for many years. *The Candlelight Patrol* is based on his experience in Saudi Arabia during the Gulf War.

Julie-Ann Simpson is an artist based in Aberdeen. Her paintings are concerned with the idea of place, frequently examining her native Scottish landscape and the narratives that occur therein.

James Sinclair began writing in his forties. His work is published in a number of anthologies and literary magazines. James is on the editorial committee of *The New Shetlander*.

Monika Stachowiak is originally from Poland. Her passion for hiking brought her to Scotland. She started making art as a hobby and now is studying Visual Communication at North East Scotland College.

Lady Thornfield is an emerging self-taught artist based in Aberdeen. As an English Literature enthusiast, the literary classics are her main inspiration, creating a kind of illustration she calls LiteratArt.

Samuel A. Verdin is an English-born writer of prose, poetry and script, currently working in Edinburgh on his first novel. For further information visit www.verdinhead.com

Loretta Diane Walker won the 2016 Phyllis Wheatley Book Award for poetry, for her collection *In This House*. She is a multiple Pushcart nominee. Walker has published three collections of poetry.

Martin Walsh, Kentish Aberdonian, retired marine biologist and renowned telepathist, relishes human and animal discourse. He's sneaking back into POTB with a [subliminal] whoop of joy.

Tez Watson has never lost that wonderment of seeing his first image appear in a shallow dish over forty years ago. He won the Maxwell Prize at the 2016 Nairn Festival.

Louise Wilford, based in South Yorkshire, has been writing poetry for several decades and has been published widely. She also writes prose fiction and educational material.

Moira Scicluna Zahra is a freelance illustrator who presently resides in Edinburgh. She has lectured graphic design in Malta for seven years as well as illustrated several published children's book.

Scottish Interest

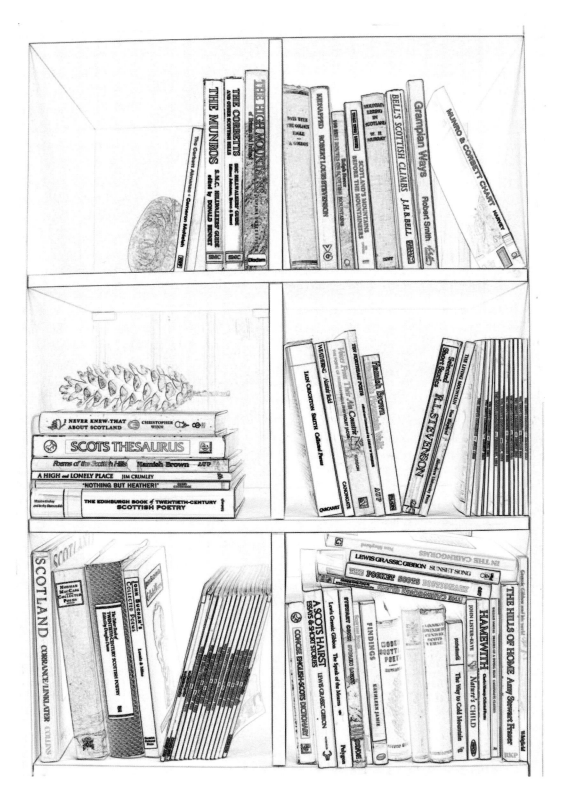

David Elder
Colour/Photography
1631 x 2400 px

PUSHING OUT THE BOAT

The Team of Volunteers who produced Issue 14:

Pushing Out the Boat [POTB] is managed and produced by this dedicated team of volunteers, and is a Scottish Charity [SCO44919]. We are indebted to **Tom Hammick** for generously allowing use of his image* on the cover of POTB14. Many thanks to **Aberdeen City Council** for financially supporting our marketing project [aided by **think PR]**; this edition was further financed by magazine sales revenue plus fundraising. We gratefully acknowledge the help of our friends & supporters, also the in-kind and reciprocal backing of our Partner organisations:

Printer: J Thomson 14-16 Carnoustie Pl, Glasgow G5 8PB

*Cover image by Tom Hammick: Violetta & Alfredo's Escape 2016, edition variable reduction woodcut, edition of 12, 160 x 120 cm, © Tom Hammick, courtesy Hammick Editions (www.hammickeditions.com) & Flowers Gallery (www.flowersgallery.com).

Email: info@pushingouttheboat.co.uk
Post: Pushing Out the Boat, c/o 23 Ferryhill Place, Aberdeen, AB11 7SE

PUSHING OUT THE BOAT

OUTLETS

Copies of the magazine (price £7 plus post/packing) can be purchased online at www.pushingouttheboat.co.uk; via our email/postal address; and from our regular outlets, whose continued support we gratefully acknowledge. This list of vendors, which is continually updated on our website, currently includes:

Aberdeen Central Library
Amigo, ARI, Forresterhill Site, Aberdeen
Bank Street Gallery, Kirriemuir
Belmont Cinema, Aberdeen
Better Read Books, Ellon
Blackwells, Old Aberdeen
Books and Beans, Belmont St, Aberdeen
Ferryhill Parish Church, Aberdeen
Gallery at Fifty Five, Stonehaven
Grassic Gibbon Centre, Arbuthnott

Hammerton Stores, Aberdeen
Michie's Pharmacy, 391 Union St, Abdn
Milton of Crathes Gallery
Newtondee Village Stores, Bieldside
Orb's Bookshop, Huntly
Peacock Visual Arts, Aberdeen
Richmond Deli, Aberdeen
The Hour Image Gallery, Forfar
Serco Northlink Ferries, Aberdeen
Waterstones, Union Bridge, Abdn

The magazines can be read at: all Aberdeen & Aberdeenshire Libraries; those of Aberdeen's Universities & Colleges; the Sanctuary Room & Roof Garden at Aberdeen Royal Infirmary. Issues 9 -12 can be read online.

Some studios and venues at NEOS 2017 [see below] will have copies of POTB 14 on sale.